D1033914

Richard Trismen
Fair Winds + Tight Lines
Ted Gerken
6/16/89

Dick:
Hope you will
enjoy the book!
Mary Gerken

Gamble at Iliamna

The story of what happened
when two Alaskans
put their entire life savings into
a frontier fly-fishing lodge

By Ted Gerken
Edited by Anne Silleck

nchor Publishing

HOMER, ALASKA

GAMBLE AT ILIAMNA

Copyright © 1988 by Anchor Publishing
All rights reserved.

No part of this work may be reproduced or transmitted in any form or by any means, electronic or mechanical, including photocopying and recording, or by any information storage or retrieval system, except as may be expressly permitted by the 1976 Copyright Act or in writing from the publisher.

Anchor Publishing
P.O. Box 30
Homer, Alaska 99603

Library of Congress Card no. 88-071248

Manufactured in the United States of America
Printed on acid-free paper

ISBN 0-945771-00-2

Acknowledgements

First, to my wife Mary, for moving to Iliamna with me in the winter of 1977 and living this story with me. Without her, none of this would have been possible.

Second, to Angus Cameron, who started me writing the manuscript with a challenge. I approached him seeking a ghost-writer for the story—his immediate response was, "Are you too lazy to do it yourself?" Since the first hand-written draft and through eight revisions, Angus has been a constant source of inspiration, guiding me through the myriad problems of organization and style, never overly-critical (although he certainly had reason to be those first few years), but steadfastly supportive.

And third, to my sister Anne Silleck who, after reading my sixth draft, announced that I needed help and volunteered to provide it herself. An accomplished editor and author, she gave me the equivalent of a college education in the art of writing—using my own manuscript as a text.

To Tom, who would have been here

INTRODUCTION

What the lucky angler fishing out of a well-run wilderness fishing lodge observes when proprietors, pilots, guides and kitchen crew go about their efficient business can be compared to what he sees when he observes an iceberg. What sticks up above the water is impressive, but it is only about one-seventh of the berg's bulk.

Similarly, what goes on under the client's eye leaves about 85% of what it takes to launch and run such a camp wholly unobserved. What goes on behind the scenes is mostly a mystery to the client.

That lucky client arises in the morning, is greeted by a cup of excellent coffee and, shortly, by a prodigious breakfast. He dons his waders, gets his kit bag and rods together and, lo, a gassed-up plane is ready with a good pilot and guide standing by. Everything else, including the makings of a super lunch, is already aboard.

The next thing the client knows, he is 30 miles away at the mouth of some beautiful wilderness river loaded with salmon, rainbow trout, char or grayling. A jet boat tethered there soon has him upriver to the first inviting pool of the day. And shortly he is into a fish. In Ted and Mary Gerken's country that fish is apt as not to be an eight or ten pound rainbow or a 12- or 15-pound salmon.

Easy, isn't it?

No, it isn't—it's damned difficult to produce such a well-oiled procedure. To run a successful fishing lodge Jack has to be a jack-of-all-trades and so does Jane. And all the trades that Jack and Jane must know are legion. They must be bank-wise in raising and using money; must savvy accounting, insurance, and tax and insurance law; and must be shrewd at buying, whether it be a case of mayonnaise or a Cessna 206. Jack must be a pilot, good on both wheels and floats and with thousands of hours of bush flying behind him. He'd better be a fair mechanic (and know how to hire and keep a good one); he must be a man good with outboards and boats, a man clever with generators, lighting, pumps, plumbing and furnaces, and most of all, maybe he had better be a keen judge of people in picking pilots and guides, and be a skilled personnel director in handling his staff.

And that's not all. He had better be a diplomat, friend and even teacher to his clients. Yes, he has to be a jack-of-all-trades and master of most, and so does Jane.

She just might not have to be a pilot, but she'd better be most of the things that Jack must be, and in addition have a paramedic's knowledge of first aid, and most important to the clients, she must be a first-rate chef, a good judge of second chefs, helpers and housekeepers, and above all a charming and thoughtful hostess who can make meals and the cocktail hour happy occasions.

Ted and Mary Gerken, co-proprietors of Iliaska Lodge, are all of these things and many others in addition ... publicity directors, advertising copy writers, versatile sales promoters, and effective correspondents.

Anything else? Yes, they'd better both be expert anglers who can teach a novice the tricks of fly fishing, and who know where the fish are at any time of the season.

One can see at once that launching and operating a fine fishing camp is an onerous job. But it is also an adventure of infinite variety, filled as it is with daily dramatic episodes often unexpected and full of surprises. But for all of its variety for Ted and Mary, it was one big, big gamble at Iliamna; the book is aptly titled.

Here is a tale of entrepreneurship on the last frontier, where boat and plane are the only ways to get outside, and where the telephone operates like a radio phone. Iliamna, 190 miles southwest of Anchorage as the raven flies, is still chiefly a Yupik Eskimo village. The only road outback, a track that follows the mighty Newhalen River whose mouth is nearby, just stops after a few miles out in the tundra. But there is a snug harbor in Lake Iliamna nearby where Ted and his pilots take off to different Shangri-las each day. They fish more than 30 rivers out of Iliaska Lodge, each of them teeming with game fish. Each day the client experiences a new aspect of the part of Iliaska Lodge that sticks out of the water. But now, with this book, the client and others who may be only arm chair adventurers may learn what goes on behind the scenes and share the history of a favorite fishing camp.

In Gamble at Iliamna, Ted tells all and brings his clients and other readers up to date about a business gamble on the tundra. There is adventure, hazard, lots of storied episodes and, yes, hard struggle, for entrepreneurship on the last frontier has peculiar problems that most businessmen are never called to face.

Through it all, of course, run exciting stories about the fly fishing that one might expect. It just may be true that fly fishing out of Iliaska Lodge is unmatched anywhere in the world. Certainly it is the only fishing lodge I ever fished from, or heard of, whose literature claims less for its fishing than reality produces. I remember well how early I learned this lesson—in my first two hours of fishing, in fact.

Ted had flown my wife and me to the now-famous Lower Talarik Creek and had left us there while he returned to the lodge to do some chores. But before he left he fished through a pool called the Rock Hole and promptly hooked, played and released a 31-inch rainbow! The wild and furious antics of that fish were a proper warning of what lay in store for my wife and me before Ted returned.

When he did return two hours later, we had hooked 10 rainbows and played and released eight. We measured each fish with a steel tape, nose to notch, before releasing. One was a "small" fish of 24 inches, probably a fish of 6 1/4 pounds. The remaining seven fish measured from 27 to 31 inches. In that "fat" season for rainbows (1979) these fish weighed from 8 1/2 to 13 pounds. Prior to that day the largest trout either of us had ever taken weighed 4 1/2 pounds.

Yes, Ted and Mary Gerken need to tell no tall tales (unless we except Ted's yarn about Bigfoot, also to be found in these pages). The salmon, trout, char, and grayling are just as big and just as numerous as the Gerkens' handsome booklet claims.

The gamble at Iliamna may have been one for Ted and Mary, yes. But this book is a lead-pipe cinch to delight and inform its readers. Indeed, it is as sure to please as the fishing at Iliaska is sure to excel.

Angus Cameron
June 1988

There's a land where the mountains are nameless,
 And the rivers all run God knows where;
There are lives that are erring and aimless,
 And deaths that just hang by a hair;
There are hardships that nobody reckons;
 There are valleys unpeopled and still;
There's a land—oh, it beckons and beckons,
 And I want to go back—and I will.

From "The Spell of the Yukon," by Robert Service

CHAPTER 1

It wasn't just the cold that caused us to huddle deeper into our parkas—after all, in Alaska 15 degrees above zero could even be considered mild for March. But add a 20-knot breeze and the chill factor plummets well below zero.

The two aircraft on the ramp that morning were in themselves a study in Alaskan aviation. My own recently repainted Cessna 180 had already seen its 21st season and glistened in the early morning sunshine. The engine had been rebuilt twice during its lifetime and had continued to run without a problem since I bought the plane five years ago. A four-place taildragger, it's still a popular bush plane in Alaska.

The other aircraft on the ramp, a C-82 or Flying Boxcar, looked old and tired. Oil streaks and temperature stains around the engine cowls revealed the 20,000 hours already logged in its colorful history. The dull gray exterior had once been a shiny silver, but now time and exposure had taken their toll. The internal frame was as clearly outlined on the aluminum skin as the ribs on a starving dog. The old war bird had been worked hard and long.

"At least one more flight," I said to myself. "I'm paying for this one." I'd chartered the Boxcar from an outfit in Anchorage to transport everything we owned from Kodiak Island to our new home in Iliamna, 140 miles to the northwest.

"Don't stand behind this thing when I start the engines," the Boxcar pilot advised before climbing into the cockpit. "She throws a little oil."

"In that case I'll start up and taxi out first." We climbed aboard the 180. As I folded my 6-foot frame into the pilot's seat, Mary, my brand-new wife and now co-pilot, checked to see that the children were safely belted into the rear seats. Mary's two daughters, 5-year-old Elizabeth and 9-year-old Angela, shared both a seatbelt and their family cat, Lightfoot, who was cautiously watching my 14-year-old son David in the other seat trying to control our exuberant beagle Louder on his lap.

"Don't worry, girls," he reassured them. "Louder never bothered our old cat in Kodiak. Give them a little time to get used to each other and they'll get along fine."

Even by Alaskan standards, the old cargo plane was full. In addition to all our furniture, it carried a brand-new Ford six-passenger pickup truck and a Toyota sedan, plus a snowmobile, an extra freezer, and my own collection of hand and power tools gathered over 20 years. I was sure we were well over the allowable 12,000 pound payload, but the two Boxcar pilots just kept stuffing in everything we carried across the ramp until they could barely close the doors.

Clear weather was forecast for the flight, but we could expect 20 to 30 knot headwinds all the way. The Kodiak airport wind sock pointed straight down the runway. "No cross winds to worry about today," I thought. "Take-off should be a snap."

The faithful Cessna engine caught on the second revolution and was soon idling smoothly as it warmed up. Completing my ground check, I eased the throttle forward, adding enough power to start us moving along the ramp toward the active runway while a cloud of blue smoke off my left wing told me the other pilot was also starting up. "He certainly wasn't fooling about burning a little extra lube oil in those old radial engines, Mary," I shouted over the noisy blast of our own engine.

Take-off was routine; the large cargo plane followed us to a cruising altitude at 8500 feet, heading northwest toward Iliamna—and the future.

Flying an airplane has been described as hours and hours of

sheer boredom interspersed with short periods of stark terror. On that cold clear day, with ceiling and visibility unlimited and the engine running smoothly under the cowl, although I couldn't admit to boredom, there was certainly no reason for terror as the panorama of Alaska passed slowly under the wings.

The winter snowcap of Kodiak and Afognak Islands shimmered in the brilliant sun, surrounded by the sparkling, white-capped, blue-gray waters of the North Pacific. Towering Mount Douglas, permanently covered with ice and with glacial ribbons running toward the sea on three sides, stood directly on our route across Shelikof Strait. The 30 miles of treacherous open water between Kodiak and the mainland, rich in marine life, this day contained an ocean-sized cargo vessel in midchannel with several commercial fishing boats hugging the shoreline, the vee of their wakes soon dissipating in the turbulent and frigid water. Even the most adventurous mariner or pilot maintains an uncommon vigil passing through or over the Strait, and I was pleased to once again reach the opposite shoreline without incident.

The cargo plane passed us at the halfway point over Mt. Douglas; 20 minutes later I heard the Boxcar pilot calling the Flight Service Station at our destination for landing advisories while we were still 15 miles out over Lake Iliamna. The flight had been a dream, without turbulence or other excitement, and as I throttled back and started my own descent, the ice-free lake glistened under our tiny craft.

Lake Iliamna is the largest lake in Alaska and the eighth largest on the North American continent. Lying southwest of Anchorage toward the Alaskan Peninsula, the lake measures almost 90 miles long and is oriented generally northeast to southwest. The southwestern end is about 25 miles wide, narrowing to less than five toward the northeast; overall, the lake covers more than a thousand square miles of surface area. A maximum depth of over one thousand feet has been recorded near the northeastern end, although the average ranges between two to three hundred feet to the southwest, making it one of the largest repositories of fresh water in the world. Islands and exposed rocks dot the surface of this enormous body of water, with several of the larger islands encompassing thousands of acres. The word *Iliamna* in the local Yupik Eskimo language means "lake with islands."

Dozens of streams—from small brooks tumbling down through snow-filled ravines to smoothly flowing creeks and large rivers steadily bring billions of gallons of clear fresh water into the lake each day. During the summer months, a few of these streams carry silty runoff from the melting glaciers to the north, creating a pale aquamarine discoloration in the clear lake water near their mouths. The Kvichak (pronounced Kwee-chak) River flows out of the lake from the southwestern end and meanders through 60 miles of tundra to the saltwater estuary of Bristol Bay, the easternmost arm of the Bering Sea.

The northeastern end of the lake is surrounded by mountains, sharply peaked and covered with snow much of the year. Higher summits with steeply sided ridges and jagged caps show that this is a new geological formation, as yet unweathered by time and the elements. Overlooking this wild and barren landscape is Mt. Iliamna at 10,016 feet above sea level. About 40 miles northeast of the lake, Mt. Iliamna is one of several active volcanoes in this part of Alaska. A constant spray of steam forms a wispy white cloud along the northeast side of the peak, where a fissure allows ice water to drain into the furnace below.

Only a hundred miles away, the southwestern shore of the lake reveals a stark difference in geology. Low hills predominate, few reaching higher than a thousand feet, all well-rounded by the glaciers of our last Ice Age. Gentle slopes glide toward wide gravel beaches, and small meandering streams carry the limited rainfall through hundreds of smaller lakes and ponds toward the big lake.

Mosses, lichens, and sedges common to the tundra dominate the vegetation to the south and west, interspersed with stands of scrub alder and a few cottonwood trees along the stream bottoms—in stark contrast to the large tracts of Sitka Spruce, alder, paper birch, and cottonwood that grow along the mountain valleys to the northeast.

The village of Iliamna lies along the western shore of the lake midway between the mountains to the north and the barren

4

tundra to the south. It is an arid wasteland of rock, gravel, and ice where the trees grow slowly, stunted by the combination of harsh climate, poor soil, and limited rainfall.

As I slowly descended over the village, we could see the small airstrip that also serves as the town's main street. Two other lodges, several homes, a community hall, and the general store line this 1500-foot strip of gravel that runs parallel to and a hundred yards from the lake shore. Pilots approaching this strip have to watch out for pedestrians (including small children), cars, trucks, dogs—and even occasionally another airplane.

Our own acquisition, Iliaska Lodge, dominated a small peninsula half a mile east of the village, its blue-green roof cheerful against the browns, grays, and whites of the surrounding area. Printed in ten-foot-tall white letters, the name ILIASKA LODGE was emblazoned on both sides of the sharply peaked roof.

"There it is, Mary. Our new home!" I shouted over the roar of the 180 and banked sharply around the structure. "We've sure come a long way in just two months."

"You're telling me," she smiled, looking down at the property and probably, like me, wondering what she was getting herself into. Marriage, a new business, a new town, a new parent for my children! All these thoughts and more coursed through my own mind and must have occurred to Mary, too, as the aircraft roared

5

past at 130 miles per hour.

Our destination this day was to be the larger, state-maintained airport four miles west of town. The Boxcar pilot had already landed on this smoother, 5000-foot runway and was slowly taxiing toward the ramp as I turned away from the village for my own approach. Gently settling the tires onto the runway, I followed the Boxcar to the gravel pad directly in front of the Flight Service Station, finally pulling the gas mixture full-lean to kill the engine.

We were home, for better or worse. The excitement of arrival masked our more basic worries, setting doubts and fears aside for awhile. Our real tests were still to come.

CHAPTER 2

The chill in Kodiak had been only a preview to the bitter cold of Iliamna. The temperature was well below zero, with a biting wind of 20 knots driving the chill factor to 50 below. As I stepped from the warm cabin of the airplane to the frozen gravel of the state airport, the moisture in my nose froze with the first breath. The exterior door handle clung to the skin of my unprotected fingers, and I quickly pulled on a pair of woolen gloves and a warm stocking cap.

As Mary bundled the youngsters and pets into the Flight Service Station, David and I headed toward the Boxcar. Dave Wilder, a local bush pilot and previous owner of the lodge, was standing beside the cargo plane talking to the Boxcar pilots and another man as we approached.

"Meet Scott Bauer," he said, turning to the lean six-footer beside him. "He's volunteered to help unload and move your things to the lodge."

Scott—as I was later to learn—worked as general handyman for the local fuel company despite holding a college degree in landscape architecture. Right now, his open smiling face and obvious enthusiasm were a welcome we hadn't expected. Volunteers can be hard to find—particularly at 50 below.

As the large cargo doors on the Boxcar slowly swung outward, exposing the entire width of the fuselage, we stood ready to catch our teetering belongings. The Ford pickup and Toyota sedan were still chained in place, but the rest of the stuff had been crammed in haphazardly, filling the hold from floor to ceiling. Taking the boxes closest to the doors, we started unloading, Mary joining us after the girls and pets were safely inside out of the cold.

Dave and Scott had brought a pickup truck with them; after filling it for the first trip to the lodge, some five miles away along a gravel road, it took another half hour for the two Boxcar pilots to expose, unchain, and unload our own truck.

We wasted little time in that frigidly cold air, fully exposed as we were to the brisk wind sweeping across the flat airport surface from the north. By the time Dave Wilder and Scott Bauer returned with their pickup, we had the Ford filled and ready to go. Quickly reloading Dave's truck, he and Scott drove off, followed by Mary and the girls in our own vehicle. Someone had to supervise the unloading at the other end or we would have had our things scattered freely in all directions by the two energetic helpers.

Meanwhile, David and I had to hustle to keep up with the two pilots. Working in the relative warmth of the cargo hold, they slid box after box toward the unloading ramp; we in turn carried them to a storage area on the frozen gravel under the tail of the cargo plane.

The unloading went considerably faster than the trucking, and we soon had a large pile of gear heaped up behind the Boxcar awaiting the return of our ground transport. Only the Toyota was still left on board—it was going on to Anchorage, to be parked at the airport where we'd need it for shopping in town. Shoving the last box down the ramp, the two pilots leaped out and slammed the cargo doors behind them, anxious to get back into the air again while their engines were still warm. Thanking them both for their help, we watched them climb back into the Boxcar and restart the engines. Then I noticed where we'd heaped our pile of belongings.

A cloud of bluish gray smoke belched from the engines, spewing hot lube oil over our precious things, coating everything in a fine globular spray that quickly congealed into a sticky film of goo. "I'm glad Mary isn't here," I said, looking around at the mess and thinking of all the dropped boxes to come. "She hates to hear me swear."

The sun had already set by the time David and I finally arrived at the lodge with our last oil-streaked load of boxes. The mercury was dropping precipitously toward the ball at the base of the thermometer and we rushed to get the last of our load into the basement. "We'll sort all this out tomorrow," I declared. "Let's get inside where it's warm."

Mary had watched us trying to wrestle the boxes out of the truck and into the lodge without dropping them, noting the ever increasing coating of goo collecting on our parkas. Whatever she had been about to say, she didn't say it. Greeting us with a sunny smile instead, she quickly pressed a mug of hot coffee into our oily, frozen hands.

Our new home was a two-story woodframe building over a full concrete basement. Originally built in 1946, the rectangular structure measured 30 by 60 feet. It was one of the largest buildings in Iliamna, with almost 5000 square feet of usable floor space under one roof. It could accommodate up to twenty guests at one time.

The main lodge was only one of several buildings scattered about the five acres of property we now owned. Of equal importance was an 8'x12' woodframe structure that housed our electric generating equipment, located fifty feet to the north of the main lodge. With no commercial power available in the community, each family had to generate their own. Two rustic cottages, an old log hut made into a workshop, two frame warehouses sheathed in rusting corrugated steel, a smokehouse, and a hundred-foot pier made up the remainder of the permanent structures.

Except for the main lodge building, which was in fairly good shape, I was soon to find that the condition of the place was marginal. All the outbuildings were in various stages of neglect. Peeling paint, sagging doors, leaking roofs, clogged septic tank—you name it and we found it somewhere on the property. On the other hand, the generator worked, and the main lodge was warm and comfortable.

Dave Wilder and his family had closed the lodge to guests a

few days before our arrival and moved into their new house. With a smile and wave, he hopped back into his own truck and vanished up the road into the night, taking Scott along with him. The paperwork necessary to transfer title had all been completed beforehand. There were no keys to worry about—there were no locks on the doors, either on the outside door or on guest bed rooms. We took over with a smile, a wave, and their wishes for good luck, the one thing we were really going to need.

Mary and I decided to remain closed for a week or more so that we could get our feet on the ground. Our own lives had changed so much in so short a time that we both felt it necessary to take more time to adjust to each other in these new surroundings before we brought strangers in to live with us.

I was 43 that year, a bit over six feet tall and 175 pounds. Slim, but no longer a skinny kid, I had managed to stay in pretty good shape despite the numerous desk jobs I'd held in the past.

A graduate of the United States Coast Guard Academy, Class of 1955, I had followed the direction and lifestyle of a Coast Guard officer for 20 years, moving from job to job and place to place as my commission and the dictates of the service demanded. I'd served on Ocean Weather Stations and Search and Rescue Cutters in the North Atlantic, spent a year of isolated duty in the Philippine Islands in charge of a Loran Station, set buoys off the coast of Florida, and then, upon transfer to Key West, rescued hundreds of Cuban refugees seeking political asylum from communist Cuba.

My last 12 years of commissioned service all involved Civil Engineering duties around the globe, including assignments in Sault Ste. Marie, Michigan; Bangkok, Thailand; Seattle; and New Orleans; all the while requesting assignment to anything in Alaska, where, I'd heard, the country was still as wild as it had been during the Gold Rush. I imagined a place where the rivers poured down from the mountains, pure and sweet and full of fish eager to strike a fly; where the caribou, moose, and bear reigned supreme over millions of uncharted acres of mountain and plain; where a man could still lose himself in the peace and beauty of wilderness untouched by human hands.

But duty called and Alaska didn't—it wasn't until I'd served my country in all its other waters that someone finally listened, and I was transferred to Kodiak Island. The U.S. Navy was decommissioning their station at Kodiak, and the Coast Guard decided to take over the entire facility and establish a new base from which to service all their units in Western Alaska. My lifelong dream had finally come true. My assignment was as the first Public Works Officer at the new base, and I was fully prepared and qualified to do the job—but my heart was already in the wilderness. To take full advantage of that small segment of paradise, I bought my first airplane.

I had been a pilot for several years, earning my first rating in a J-3 Piper Cub in 1965. A commercial license, instructor's rating, and instrument rating followed over the next few years using funds available through the G.I. Bill. After four months on the job at Kodiak, I took a commercial flight to Seattle, bought a used Cessna 180 on floats (with wheels for winter flying), arranged for instruction, received my float rating in the new plane, and took off solo for Alaska—the next day!

Then I felt prepared to "do it all." An indefatigable fly fisherman from childhood, I could now pit my skills against the salmon, steelhead, char, and trout of Kodiak and the nearby mainland. An enthusiastic hunter, I could now stalk the bear, moose, elk, sheep, caribou, and deer of the region and fill our freezer with the tastiest of wild game. And best of all, I now had an airplane to get there with, an aerial taxi at my own disposal. With the flick of an ignition key, the remotest parts of Alaska were now within reach.

If it wasn't, fortunately, too good to be true, it was, unfortunately, too good to last. After three years, the Coast Guard decided they needed me elsewhere. My first wife was ecstatic—she'd hated Alaska ever since her first winter and couldn't wait to get back to civilization and into the thick of things again.

But elsewhere—I suspected Washington, D.C.—even with a promotion to Captain was a bit too thick for me and I put in for voluntary early retirement instead. Why move on when I was already where I'd always wanted to be? As for the Coast Guard, I would have to learn to live without it—and yes, without my wife, too, if it came to that.

It did. She left me for the States for three and four weeks at a time after my retirement officially began on June 30, 1975, leaving our three half-grown sons with me to care for during her prolonged absences.

The next day, July 1st, I began a new career as City Manager for the City of Kodiak. If I'd expected the civilian world to be as sure and steady as the Coast Guard, local politics in Kodiak quickly disenchanted me. After one year I'd already outlasted most of my many predecessors. Exactly a year and seven months after taking office, I was fired. Shortly after that my wife and I divorced.

Within a month I proposed to my ex-secretary from City Hall, Mary, who'd been raised in Alaska since the age of three and loved it even more than I did. She cooked like an angel; danced like a dream; worked like a beaver (she'd been brought up on a homestead)—she even liked to fish and hunt. When we saw an ad in *The Anchorage Times* offering this lodge for sale, it didn't take us very long to make up our minds to buy it.

So here we were, newlyweds setting out on a new adventure that promised everything we'd always dreamed of: freedom, wilderness, self-sufficiency—and fish!

CHAPTER 3

Starting right out with 16-hour days, Mary and I went to work, she concentrating on the interior of the main lodge while I sorted through the rest of our rundown estate. Although we'd planned on staying closed awhile longer, there were no other lodges open in the village that winter. Just one week after we moved in, our first guest arrived—by helicopter and in a blinding snowstorm. We had about two minutes advance warning by telephone.

"Hello, Ted, this is Howard out at Flight Service. I've got a helicopter approaching, and the pilot says he needs a place to stay tonight."

I looked outside at the snow swirling around the lodge. "What's a guy doing out in this stuff?" I asked. "Visibility can't be more than a few hundred feet down here."

"He knows it. He just passed over the field a few minutes ago and is trying to navigate by following the road to your place. Should be getting pretty close by now. Wants to know if you're open."

"Tell him we'll open up for him." Dropping the receiver, I called to Mary and ran to open the drapes on the road side of the lodge. Sure enough, there was a flashing red beacon just visible through the blowing snow, with the outline of a Bell Jet Ranger hovering beneath the light.

Pilot Dick Izold of Anchorage safely edged past the generator shack, hovering a mere ten feet in the air as he tried to follow the edge of the road. Throwing on a parka and boots, I hit the front stairs running as he came around the corner of the lodge, the helicopter dead center over the gravel driveway and slowly moving toward the frozen, snow-covered lawn. Down drafts from the large rotor whipped billows of drifted snow back into the air, blinding the pilot. Now only 75 feet away, the helicopter vanished in a blizzard of its own making.

Running out under the circling rotors until the pilot could see me, I waved my arms to indicate he should keep going toward the lawn and set her down there. Only a veteran pilot could have made such a landing. Relying solely on his instruments to maintain flight, he waited until the heavy downwash from his rotors cleared the area below, then slowly descended until the skids of his Jet Ranger touched the bare ground right in the middle of our front yard.

"I'll stay here a week if necessary, but I'm not taking off into that stuff again," Dick Izold said as he stepped out of the cabin. "Sure appreciate you folks opening up for me." Heavily swathed in an insulated flight suit and parka, he had been flying through the storm for the past half hour, and the strain of concentration still marked the ruggedly handsome face of this experienced bush pilot.

"You're our first guest. Come on in and get some hot coffee. You look like you could use a cup," I said—and with that, we were in business.

Our second guest, a young Public Health Service Doctor on his rounds among the native villages in the region, arrived only a few minutes later in a jeep he had borrowed from the local native health aide. Dean Drescher shed his parka and boots in the entryway, opened the inner door, and called, "Anybody here?"

"Sure are. Come on in."

Dean soon joined Dick and me at the table. "By God, that's miserable out there. Sure am thankful you people are accepting guests."

"We weren't until a little while ago. Meet Dick Izold, pilot of that helicopter on the front lawn. He only beat you by minutes."

"What do you take in your coffee, Doctor?" Mary asked, approaching with the steaming coffee pot and a handful of extra

14

mugs.

"Just black, Ma'am. Hot and black. A good contrast to that frigid and white just outside the window," he answered. "Are we really your first guests?"

"The very first."

Dick immediately stood up, reached into a pocket for his billfold, and took out a one-dollar bill. "Then it's my privilege to give you your first dollar," he declared, handing the bill to Mary. "I can't imagine a more fitting way to start than helping us on such a lousy day." With full cups, we toasted the start of Iliaska Lodge under the Gerkens' proprietorship.

The weather cleared overnight and we woke to a world benign and brilliant, the snow stretching white and innocent beside the still gray mirror of the lake. A few white tendrils of clouds on the eastern horizon marked the only flaw in an otherwise solid blue sky, and there was not so much as a breath of wind to betray the howling blizzard of the day before. It was a world serene and beautiful—except for the helicopter standing in the center of a brown patch of frozen grass in our front yard.

"Thanks again for everything," the pilot called, climbing back into his machine.

"Glad to have you," I said, stepping back to watch his flight preparations from the shelter of the doorway. "Drop in anytime."

Doctor Drescher left a short while later in the jeep. We had decided to charge fifty dollars per night for room and board, and thus earned our first hundred—and one—dollars.

We were alone again for the rest of the week until another stranded group of aviators dropped in because of bad weather. A commercial charter pilot was bound for Bristol Bay and had three passengers with him—including an Alaska State Trooper and his prisoner, a native from one of the neighboring villages.

"I would like one room for the two of us," said Officer Gilson, most impressive in his full uniform and standing a good 6'4" in the lodge entryway.

I glanced at his prisoner—a slender 5'4" but charged with almost killing his wife in a drunken brawl the previous day. "I wouldn't have it any other way, Officer," I said. "Let me show you to your room."

15

And so it went for the next few months—not a lot of business but reasonably steady at three or four guests a week. One thing you could say for it—we certainly got to know what was going on in the community.

CHAPTER 4

L odges in rural areas of the United States can be great places to visit. Quaint and old-fashioned, they exemplify the slower life of a past generation—local conversation liberally sprinkled with a little dry humor, warm and friendly hospitality, family-style home cooking. Surrounded by the natural beauty of the countryside, it is only here that the traveler finds the peace of gently lapping waters, the majesty of mountains thrusting ice-covered peaks against the sky, the breadth and wonder of prairie and tundra rolling endlessly to the horizon.

But if our visitors were surrounded by peace and majesty and wonder, Mary was swamped under piles of dirty sheets and stacks of dirty dishes while I was kept running from one odd job to another trying to catch up with all the carpentry, plumbing, and electrical repairs that the former owners had let slide. All our money, every last cent, was now sunk in the lodge and there were times when it seemed as if we were slowly sinking in after it. If we weren't already in over our heads, we soon would be.

Up to now, the lodge had been run like a hotel, providing room and board plus taxi service to and from the two local airports. Our dream was to run an exclusive fly-out fishing lodge, but for now, with the bills rolling in regularly, there was no other alternative but to keep on going—even though we soon realized that continued operation as a hotel would drive us, exhausted, right to the poorhouse. There just weren't enough year-round travelers in this remote part of Alaska.

"What do you think, Mary?" I asked her one night after the last guest had finally gone upstairs to bed. Mary still had an hour's work left in the kitchen preparing for tomorrow, but she looked as if she'd been worked half to death already—her face drawn in deep lines and her eyes dull and lifeless. "Is it really worth it? Maybe we should just give up now while we still have something left."

"What? What do we have left?" Mary wanted to know, unloading the dishwasher for the third time that night, slamming pots and pans left and right. "A home? A family? A marriage?"

"At least we have each other," I said.

Mary looked at me with infinite pity. "No we don't, Ted," she said. "What we have is a lodge. That's all we have. Now go away and leave me alone because I have a batch of sourdough to get started for biscuits in the morning."

"Let them eat toast," I said, taking her firmly in hand and carrying her off to bed. She fell asleep before I could even get the shoes off her feet.

One day when I was out in the shack checking the generator, I took a closer look at the other machine there. According to the name plate, it was manufactured by the Witte Engine Company and must have been over forty years old. We needed a backup generator in case our good one malfunctioned, but this one didn't look as if it would ever run again.

The first thing to do was to try to find some sort of instruction book. The next time I drove into the village, I asked Len McMillen, the local storeowner, if he knew where I could find one.

"You can borrow mine," he said. "But that thing hasn't run in years."

To which Mary's comment, when I told her that night, was: "You know we're in the back of beyond when everybody knows whose engines are running."

After studying the manual awhile and comparing the diagrams with the machine, I found there were some pieces missing. I recalled Dave Wilder saying that the missing parts might be in the shop or maybe the warehouse; after some rummaging and a lot of makeshift effort with the tools I had at hand, I managed to put it all back together.

This particular model was started by hand, with the receiver for the crank handle mounted on a huge flywheel. The generator itself was driven by a belt from the engine flywheel; the whole thing weighed nearly a ton. The starting instructions read as follows: 1) release the compression with the operating handle on the cylinder head; 2) insert the starting crank in its receiver on the flywheel; 3) start turning the crank, building up speed and momentum with the engine and flywheel together; and 4) restore compression.

According to the book, at that point the engine should start, using the momentum of the spinning flywheel to continue turning the engine through enough revolutions for ignition.

That's what the book said—in reality, the thing continued turning for only two or three revolutions and stopped dead. I then tried to continue turning the crank against the compression of that single cylinder. Again it wouldn't start, although I could usually get six to eight strokes before the compression overcame both me and the momentum of the heavy flywheel.

At that point, the manual became a little vague; 5) If the engine has not started, check to see that both the fuel and air supply are adjusted properly, and repeat the starting process—apparently until you drop dead of exhaustion. My personal best was four tries in succession before having to stop and rest.

It was an occupation for a strong back and a weak mind, but I persevered, even though I'd begun to doubt if the thing would ever start. It would fire once or twice and then quit, leaving me not only discouraged but with an arm that felt like lead and a devastating backache.

"I give up," I told Mary, coming into the kitchen after one more try at the beast, my arm so sore I couldn't even lift up the coffee cup Mary quickly poured for me. "It's never going to work. Nothing's ever going to work. We were fools to think we could ever make a go of it here."

"You look like you could use that coffee," Mary said, too busy with dinner to stop and argue. "Maybe you should pour some down that machine of yours."

I took a sip of coffee, ignoring such foolishness.

"It gets you up and moving in the morning, so why not old Witte?"

"If that's all the sympathy I get..." I started, but suddenly I realized she was partly right. The old engine probably did need a good swift kick to get it going again. Forsaking the coffee, but with a quick peck on the cheek for my wife, I ran out the door headed for the shop and the spray can of starter fluid I remembered seeing a few days before.

The old Witte coughed, sputtered—and caught, its one-cylinder engine slowly revving up to its operating speed of 800 rpm. When I checked the electrical leads, it was generating at exactly 115 volts.

"I did it!" I cried, racing back to the kitchen to tell Mary. "I did it, Mary! It started! It works!"

"We did it," Mary answered—and later that night, lying in bed listening to the steady *chuf-chuf-chuf* of the old Witte cranking away out in the generator shack, I knew Mary was right—we had done it, we could do it, we were here to stay!

CHAPTER 5

It wasn't long before Mary's reputation as a cook spread throughout the area, and people started stopping by just for the meals. Much of our early business came from stranded pilots forced to stay in Iliamna overnight due to bad weather; soon even the airport operators at the local Flight Service Station were recommending Mary's cooking.

A pinch of this, a splash of that—and even the plainest dishes become mouthwatering delicacies in Mary's hands. Scorning exact measurements, she can lift the lid of a pot and know almost by the smell what the dish needs; she goes through cookbooks tasting the recipes as she reads them.

But if Mary's cooking is an art, her baking is divine—I've often told her I would have married her for her cinnamon rolls alone. She starts from scratch and insists on using only the best ingredients—something of a problem when the nearest supermarket is a few hundred air-miles away.

"Ted, I've got a problem. I want to be able to serve those four Italians a real Italian dinner tomorrow night. The spaghetti recipe calls for Prosciutto ham and freshly ground Parmesan cheese. On your trip to town today could you stop by a grocery store and pick some up for me?"

I'd never heard of Prosciutto ham. "You'd better write that down for me, Mary. Are you sure I can get that kind of ham in Anchorage? And that cheese?"

"I hope so. If not, they'll have to eat my own spaghetti."

21

"Nothing wrong with that. The kids and I sure like it." I try to be encouraging; nobody benefits from her cooking more than I do.

"Never mind the blarney, sweetheart. Just see if you can find it and call me if not so I can change the menu."

Late that afternoon I called from town. "Mary, I've been to four stores looking for your Italian cooking stuff. Three of them tried to be helpful—they have grated Parmesan cheese and suggested you use American bacon as a substitute for the ham. The other guy just laughed and asked me if I thought I was in New York."

"I was afraid of that," Mary answered.

"There's only four hours of daylight left, and it takes two for the flight home. If you want me to go on looking, I'll have to spend the night here."

Mary never liked me spending the night alone in Anchorage—we never knew when something else might go wrong at the lodge, and it was always better when the chief mechanic was around. "I'll change the menu, Ted. Come on back."

"Are you sure? I could take a little more time."

"Yes," Mary said. "I've been thinking about it, and decided to stick to the kind of cooking I do best and not try to imitate others. Nothing wrong with good, wholesome Alaskan cooking."

Mary could do no better than go with her feelings on this matter. She'd learned scratch cooking from one of the best cooks in Alaska—her own mother, Martha Wickersham. While Mary was growing up in Homer, Martha ran a small restaurant in town called The Family Cafe. Mary and her four sisters all took their turns at waitressing and short-order cook, but only Mary progressed to soup and salad preparation and finally to dinner chef, spelling her mother on Martha's few days off. Mary learned the secrets of quantity cooking as the popular restaurant flourished: the use of spices and condiments, the secrets of homemade soups and salad dressings, the mysteries of gravies and special sauces. When she declared there was nothing wrong with good Alaskan cooking, I cheered her decision.

The month of May flashed by as Mary and I worked feverishly to get ready for the summer. To raise a little extra cash, I worked days as a carpenter for a local contractor who was putting up a small restaurant alongside the gravel runway in Iliamna. Evenings and weekends I devoted to the lodge, where I was kept busy with the airplane. One weekend I flew it to Kodiak, where my son Tom and I converted it back to a seaplane, removing the wheels and installing the large floats we had left stored in the city.

When flying over a land dotted with hundreds of lakes, rivers, and creeks—where airstrips are few and far between—there's a degree of confidence and security gained by operating on floats instead of wheels. Many of these bodies of water can be used as emergency landing areas should something go wrong with the aircraft or should weather conditions deteriorate badly. Having the aircraft on floats is also essential for a fishing lodge, so that I could ferry our guests to the best fishing spots.

Refloating the plane in the spring is relatively easy. This year the hard part—since the previous owners had not run a seaplane—was constructing a gas station on the pier (including tanks, pump, piping, and filters) so that I could safely moor and refuel the plane while it was in the water.

Meanwhile, in addition to preparing all the meals, Mary scrubbed and waxed the floors, dusted and polished the furniture, and washed all the ceilings and walls, until the whole lodge fairly squeaked with cleanness. By June we were ready.

For staff we had Mary's two daughters and my three sons, who arrived in early June for the summer. At nineteen, Bill was the oldest and enrolled at the University of Alaska in Fairbanks, ready to start his sophomore year in the fall. Tom at eighteen had just graduated from high school in Kodiak, where his younger brother David had just finished his freshman year. Angela had just completed fourth grade in Iliamna and five-year-old Elizabeth was scheduled to start first grade in the fall. Not, perhaps, the most competent staff for a fishing lodge—but ready and willing and able.

But success depends on sales, and where were the clients?

Mary and I were ready; the lodge was ready; fishing was extraordinarily good—but where were the fishermen? The few anglers who did stay with us that June used the lodge for hotel services only. Instead of chartering me to guide them to the fishing streams, they had the local air taxi operator take them out each day—a throwback to previous years that was going to take some real effort to overcome.

The previous owners had approached a travel agent in Anchorage, trying to expand business during the forthcoming fishing season, and we flew into town in April to see him. His office was on the basement level of the Post Office Mall on 4th Avenue, an area of town frequented by drunks, prostitutes, and a few tourists during the summer months of July and August. Two girls were working behind a counter littered with travel brochures from points around the world. Mr. Jackson's desk was in the rear, shielded by a portable screen from the rest of the office.

Carter Jackson was a small man with a thin face marked with small irregular skin discolorations. He walked with a limp, favoring his left leg. I didn't much like the look of him but there wasn't time to change horses now.

He had prepared a travel brochure for Iliaska Lodge; after making some minor changes to the text, we approved the draft and asked him to expedite printing. The season was almost upon us and we needed any advertising we could get.

"You folks don't need to worry about a thing," Mr. Jackson assured us. "Anchorage is expecting a hundred thousand visitors this summer, and our own advertising campaign is well underway to attract a lot of this business. We'll fill your lodge easily."

I guess we believed him because we wanted to. Mary and I had so little experience operating a sportfishing lodge that it was frightening to think we had invested our entire life's savings in it.

Fortunately, we had some business from the State of Alaska, which had contracted to make major improvements to the gravel road system in the area. The work had started the summer before and a crew of five to six men had stayed at the lodge with the previous owners, abandoning the project during the winter. They had moved back in with us shortly after Memorial Day to begin work as soon as the ground thawed. The steady income they provided brought some relief to our burgeoning financial problems, and by mid-June we were even able to pay some of our already complaining creditors.

But things really started looking good when the Fire Fighting Division of the Bureau of Land Management called us to ask about lodging for their firemen and support personnel. Lightning strikes in the dry tundra had started several fires in Southwestern Alaska, and the Bureau had decided to establish a semi-permanent base camp at Iliamna, finally selecting Iliaska Lodge as their site. So by the 20th of June we had almost a full house of heavy-equipment operators, BLM bureaucrats, and firefighters.

With a workload like that, we had to hire another helper and found a young lady in the village to help Mary with the housekeeping chores. Bill was working with me each day, while Tom and David alternated between helping me outside and Mary inside. The system worked out pretty well until the day Mary decided to make homemade pizza as a treat for the men.

We had a full house of 20 guests already, plus a few extra smokejumpers sleeping on cots in the basement. Mary had dinner preparations well underway when the chief firefighter strolled into the kitchen.

"Say, Mary, do you think you could feed a few more people tonight?"

"Sure," she said, thinking a few meant one or two late arrivals.

"Headquarters just called and said they were sending down three more crews. I'll have to bivouac them at the airport but they'll need feeding."

"THREE MORE CREWS!" Mary said. "That's 30 more mouths!"

"It's just for tonight," the chief apologized, edging back toward the door. "And breakfast tomorrow morning."

Mary looked around her kitchen, at the preparations for pizza that already covered all her workspace, and immediately began organizing an assembly line in her mind. "Okay," she said, rolling up her sleeves to get another batch of dough started at once, "we'll do it. But it will take at least an hour before we can be ready for the first crew. My oven only holds three pizzas at a time, so figure, if it's six o'clock now, the first delivery will be 7:30, the second at 8:00, the third at 8:30, and so on."

"Thanks, Mary," the Chief was grateful for anything he could get. "I know it's a lot to ask. If you want to use Bisquick or something, it's okay, they won't know the difference."

Mary gave him a look he regretted. "Please tell Ted I'm going to need some more help in here. He's in the shop."

Five minutes later Tom and David showed up in the kitchen, where Mary and Angie were already at work. "Dad said you needed more help. He's almost got that new voltage regulator hooked up on the generator. He'll be here soon. What can Dave and I do?"

"Wash your hands, both of you, then Tom, you slice the pepperoni and onions. Angie is grating the cheese. David, get those cookie sheets out from under the stove and grease them. Lay them out along the counter and sprinkle a little of this corn meal on each one."

Fortunately pizza dough doesn't have to rise. Mary already had the dough ready and was working on the sauce.

"How many pans do you want greased, Mary?"

"All of them. There should be four there."

In 30 minutes of concerted effort, all the ingredients for 65 servings of Mary's homemade pizza lined every counter in the kitchen. "Okay, gang, here's how we do it. I'll lay out the dough. David, you spread the sauce and sprinkle the chopped olives from this gallon jar on top. Tom, you put on the pepperoni and onion slices, and Angie sprinkles on the cheese."

"That doesn't leave much for Dad."

"Don't worry about your father. He gets to deliver them to the airport while we cook. Now let's get busy."

As Mary slipped the first three pans into the stove, she suddenly realized that she couldn't serve directly from them since they had to be used in the oven over and over again. "Tom, go out to the shop and find me some plywood about the size of the cookie sheets. We'll have to slide the pizzas onto the wood for the trip to the airport. Angela, go downstairs and get me that roll of brown paper by the ping-pong table. We'll cover the sheets of plywood with paper, slide the pizzas onto them, and then wrap each one in aluminum foil. That should keep them fairly warm in the truck."

"Who gets the first batch, Mary? The airport crew or us?"

"First batch goes to the airport; second to our guests here; third to the airport; and so on,"—not particularly welcome news to the three hungry helpers smelling the savory odor of fresh pizza coming from the oven. "Don't worry, there should be enough for everybody; it's just going to take awhile."

As each batch of pizza came out of the oven, it was served up just as Mary had programmed it. My half-hour trips to the airport were timed to coincide with every other batch of pizza from Mary's small oven. The Chief Firefighter accompanied me on the first trip to help unload and serve the dinners, which included a salad, apple juice, and hot coffee. After that he decided to stay at the lodge and eat his own dinner—the smell of hot pizza in the truck's cab was too much for him, so I made the next four trips alone.

They were still at it in the kitchen when I got back from my last trip at 10:15, cleaning up for the 65 breakfasts due at dawn the next morning.

"If I should ever tell you I'm planning to make pizza again, Ted," Mary said as we were getting into bed at last, "please just shoot me. You'll know I've gone mad."

CHAPTER 6

It was the 24th of June; bright sunshine filled the day, with only a few small puffy white clouds drifting across the azure blue canopy overhead. A light breeze gently rippled the smooth surface of the water in front of the lodge; the absence of swells meant the weather was calm over the entire lake.

For the third day in a row we had a full lodge of 20 guests. To celebrate, I suggested to Mary we go exploring for good fishing spots in the airplane. Mary had started fly-fishing that spring; not only could she get more practice at it, but she could also get away from the kitchen for awhile. So while she packed a lunch, I went down to the airplane to preflight and fuel it for our day off.

By noon we were headed north, flying through clear skies and smooth air, with the sun behind us brightly illuminating each mountain crest. Our short Alaskan spring had burst into summer and the tundra was radiant with the colors of millions of wild flowers. Several shades of green filled each canyon and river valley, while sparkling streams danced in the bright sun. On the higher elevations, sheep, moose, and caribou trails crisscrossed the barren hills, their foot-wide tracks clearly outlined against the shale deposits on each slope.

When we reached the Mulchatna River, I reduced power to descend for a closer look at the water. The river was high—not over its banks, but the water was discolored by glacial runoff upstream somewhere. I circled the river once at an altitude of a few hundred feet and headed upstream; we would probably find some good fishing above the source of the runoff.

The confluence of the Mulchatna and Chilikadrotna Rivers was only 20 miles away. Although the Chilikadrotna is a tributary of the Mulchatna, today it carried the heavier flow, its glacial waters rushing into those of the Mulchatna and stirring up a roiling aquamarine flood. Five hundred feet below the junction, in the middle of the river, the root structure of a large spruce tree had caught in the riverbed and rode there breasting the rushing waters, its trunk and branches trailing downstream.

Just upstream of the junction a large gravel bar half overgrown with alder and willow split the Mulchatna into two halves. Here the water looked smooth and clear; it would provide a good place to moor the airplane. After three inspection

passes over the area, I decided to land just below the confluence, heading upstream. Touching down on the river, I taxied
into the five-knot current until we reached the gravel bar. The
airplane came to a smooth stop as the floats beached on a silty
bar, and we climbed out to inspect our little piece of paradise.

A light breeze blowing upstream held the plane against the
bar, so, without another thought, I got our fishing tackle and
lunch out of the back seat and waded toward the beach where
Mary was waiting. After a leisurely lunch in the sun, we started
fishing.

After fishing awhile but catching nothing, Mary decided to
take a few pictures of the spot. Almost on cue, a fully grown cow
moose weighing close to 800 pounds appeared along the opposite bank. She posed very nicely with her two front feet in the
water before slowly wandering away upstream, nibbling on the
tender spring shoots of willow as she went.

I started fishing in the calm water on the side of the bar
where I'd parked the airplane. After ten minutes without a
strike, I moved around the bar to fish the swiftly flowing water
in the main channel, standing knee-deep in the river casting for
the rainbow trout, arctic char, and arctic grayling I thought to
be there. I used my favorite eight-foot bamboo rod and a small
streamer fly I had tied myself.

"Hey Ted, turn around and say cheese," Mary called from the
gravel bar.

As I turned to give her a big smile, I saw behind her our
airplane slowly begin to float out of the calm water of our little
haven toward the rushing current in the main channel. The
wind had shifted and strengthened and was now blowing in
strong gusts that were pushing the plane away from us.

"MARY, THE AIRPLANE!" I yelled, rushing out of the
water. Dropping my fly rod on the gravel bar, I charged into the
river on the opposite side. The water surged into my hip boots
as I lunged into deep water; soon I was waist deep and
floundering. Caught in the faster current, the plane began
moving even more rapidly away from me. In desperation—
knowing I couldn't wade any further anyway—I struck out
swimming.

I'm a reasonably good swimmer but never had I tried to swim with hip boots on. It wasn't long before I was in over my head. Normally I could easily swim the 15 feet to the plane in a few seconds, but, hampered by those bulky boots, it was all I could do just to stay afloat.

Now the current began relentlessly sweeping me downstream along with the airplane. I quickly realized the plane was gone and I'd better start thinking about saving myself. The nearest shore line was about 20 feet away and heavily overgrown with alder trees; paddling and kicking toward it, I managed to reach out and grab one of the overhanging branches as I swept by.

Holding on against the pull of the current as the river rushed by, I watched the airplane float downstream directly into the waiting arms of the spruce tree.

The right float struck the stump and roots and lifted clear of the river, forcing the left float underwater and tipping the whole airplane as if in a steep left turn. The left wingtip plunged into the riverbed and the plane held solidly there, nose high and tail down, pinned to the stump by the powerful force of the current.

Pulling myself onto the bank, I walked back up the shore. Waving to Mary still standing on the bar that I was still alive, I started looking for a way to get back to the gravel bar myself.

Finding a 20-foot log large enough to hold my weight, I yanked it free from a pile of driftwood and dragged it back into the water, pushing it ahead of me as once more I waded into the river. I hadn't noticed the cold before but I noticed it now—a bone-chilling 43 degrees. Gasping for breath, I held onto the log with one arm and paddled across with the other, my hip boots dragging along below and my teeth chattering all the way.

By now it was almost three in the afternoon. The day was still fairly warm and sunny; fortunately, the wind that had blown the airplane off the bar had now subsided to a whisper. We had only the clothes we were wearing—wet in my case— and no food other than a few scraps left from lunch. All our emergency supplies were still in the airplane; more importantly, our Emergency Locator Transmitter (ELT) was also still on board, and it had to be turned on as soon as possible to let others know where to find us. There was just no way around it—I had to get back on board, the sooner the better.

We decided to find a log that I could sit on and ride downriver toward the plane. How I was to get back to Mary was not discussed, nor the possibility that I might not make it to the plane at all. Without hipboots, I could probably swim to shore somewhere.

As the current rushed me toward the stranded craft, I had only a few seconds to decide how to get aboard, realizing a miscalculation on my part could either pin me alongside the submerged float or sweep me away downriver. A hundred feet upstream of the plane I launched myself into the river, now swimming strongly.

Passing directly over the partially submerged float and under the aircraft hull, I grabbed for a float strut and hung on, the huge stump now only inches from my head. Hanging there a minute to catch my breath, I climbed up over the cabin, waving to Mary that I'd made it.

I had to swim that frigid river three more times to get back to Mary with the emergency supplies. She had a fire going when I returned and brewed up some tea made from the leaves of the fireweed plant she'd found growing on the gravel bar. After six trips in that cold water, coupled with the exertion of swimming, she was worried about hypothermia and insisted I sit down in the warm sun to rest and drink some hot tea. At least, now, the activated ELT was transmitting our wail of distress into the Alaskan skies and we could camp there comfortably until someone found us.

It was approaching six o'clock when we heard an airplane approaching from downriver and quickly loaded more wood on the fire, hoping the smoke would attract the pilot's attention. Already homing in on our emergency beacon, the pilot spotted us on his second pass and dropped a note: "Helicopter coming— stay there." An hour later we heard the *whomp whomp whomp* of the rescue craft in the still evening air.

The next day a larger cargo helicopter lifted our plane from the river, but it was three more weeks before it was back in the air under its own power.

I have never since failed to tie down an airplane, no matter how balmy the day.

CHAPTER 7

Living in such an isolated spot creates its own problems. With the nearest city over a hundred miles away—and then accessible only by air—even a minor medical problem can become a major headache, particularly when bad weather prohibits flying.

The beagle we'd brought with us to Iliamna, a gift from a friend on Kodiak Island, soon worked her way into all our hearts. Named Louder, for a persistently lamentable voice when tied outside, she came into heat in April. Rather than risk the chance of her mating with one of the local huskies, we took her back to Kodiak for breeding with a friend's dog—an old trail-wise beagle with a keen nose, tenacious determination afield, and pleasant disposition at home.

Mid-morning one day in late June Louder started into labor. We were busy with a lodge full of guests, but when we left the dog alone in the bedroom, she'd climb from the low-sided cardboard box we'd prepared for her and waddle out to the front room. She obviously wanted company in her hour of need so Mary sent five-year-old Liz back to the bedroom to 'dog sit'—we certainly didn't want the puppies born on our front room carpet.

Half an hour later, Liz came running down the hall into the kitchen. "Mommy, Mommy, Mommy," she cried. "Louder had a puppy. LOOK!"

Holding out her hands, Liz showed us Louder's firstborn. She'd barely allowed the dog time to sever the umbilical cord before she'd scooped up the puppy and rushed out to show her own Mom. Still wet and slimy, half in and half out of its amniotic sack, the one-minute-old puppy lay squirming in her hands.

"Oh Liz, isn't that a pretty one," Mary said. "But we'd better take it back to Louder, honey, so she can finish cleaning it up. She probably misses it."

Poor Louder was almost ready to start on number two but went immediately to work licking the first as soon as Liz gave it back.

Louder gave birth to five healthy puppies that day, three males and two females. For the next week, the mother was constantly in attendance on them. She would only leave the puppies long enough to eat and drink and go outside, quickly returning to the box after each absence, flopping down on her side to offer her ravenous brood another taste of dinner.

Eight days later, I was sitting at the dining room table when I saw Louder half-walk and half-drag herself from the bedroom out to the living area and collapse at my feet under the table. "There's something wrong with Louder!" I called to Mary, who was in the kitchen. Mary came running and knelt down beside me to get a closer look.

"Oh my God, it's milk fever," she said. "When I was a girl, we had a dog on the homestead who did the same thing after she had puppies. Better call the vet."

Although lacking all other utilities in Iliamna, we did have a telephone that worked most of the time. The closest veterinarian, however, lived in Homer, about 120 air miles to the east. It would take over an hour to fly there in the 180.

"Bring the dog in immediately," the vet said. "It sounds like milk fever. The dog needs a calcium injection as soon as possible or her chances of survival aren't good. Only 50% of these cases live, even with the injection."

"But doctor, I'm calling from Iliamna," Mary said, her voice full of tears. "Isn't there something we can do? The weather is terrible here and we can't fly today."

"Do you have any powdered milk?" he asked. "How about honey? Do you have any honey?"

"We have some Milkman," Mary said, naming a brand of dried milk. "And honey, too."

"Mix some powdered milk, honey, and water to a thin paste and see if you can get it down her throat," the vet said. "It's your only chance."

"We'll try," Mary said. "Anything else?"

"If she recovers, don't let the puppies near her again. You'll have to feed them by hand from now on. You can use a formula of half evaporated milk and half corn syrup."

Louder was now lying completely helpless on her side, her body shaking terribly and all four legs rigidly streched out from her body. Her tongue lolled from her slack jaws and her eyes stared blankly into space. The prognosis certainly didn't look good.

All work was abandoned as we knelt by the diningroom table, slowly trickling the thin white paste into Louder's mouth, dabbling our fingers in the milk mixture and holding them over her open jaws to let the liquid drip slowly down her throat. Most of the paste ended up on floor; in her seizure, Louder had lost control over the muscles in her throat.

Fortunately, some of the formula made it into her stomach, but it was almost two hours before the dog started to show signs of recovery. Gradually the seizures became less violent, the shaking stopped, and her eyes came back into focus—but we didn't relax until we saw the tip of her tail begin to wag as she started to lap some of the formula off our fingers with her own tongue.

As soon as she could stagger to her feet, Louder headed back to her puppies. We steered her into the girls' room instead, where we kept a close watch on her the rest of the evening.

Dinner was late that night. As the firefighters and road crew came in after work, expecting to find a hot meal waiting for them and a quiet evening of reading or cards, they walked instead into bedlam. The puppies by now were all squealing with hunger.

Louder was barking furiously to be let out so she could feed them. The children were trying to dribble formula into the puppies' mouths but they were no substitute for Louder, and little Liz, distraught and crying, was running back and forth between the puppies and the bedroom where Louder was imprisoned. Mary was trying to cook dinner in between running back and forth checking on Louder, the puppies and the children—while I had to make a trip to the airport for even more guests. The commercial flight had made it in, despite the weather.

"I'm sorry," I apologized to one old bulldozer operator after returning to the lodge. He'd just come in himself, tired, hungry, and frowning over the commotion. "We'll be back to normal soon. Our dog was sick and we have to feed the puppies by hand."

He was a tall, heavyset man with a reddish face and balding gray hair. "Bring them in here," he growled. "We'll all take a hand."

Carrying the boxful of puppies out to the front room, I set it down in the middle of the rug. Soon all five puppies—eyes still firmly closed and weighing less than a pound—were eagerly sucking milk from the gentle fingers of firefighters, bushpilots, and roadcrew alike. Dipping their hands into the milk formula, they let the pups suck it off their fingers, slowly lowering their hands into the dish of milk until the puppies began to drink directly from the dish, enough at last to satisfy their hunger. Afterwards, where Louder would have licked each one to stimulate digestion, we had to gently rub their little bellies until they fell asleep in our hands.

For months afterward, the dozer operator was still calling up and chatting about the weather and the lodge, the family and the fishing. One time, I kept him talking for almost five minutes before I mentioned the puppies and how they were doing.

CHAPTER 8

At the time we moved to Iliamna, the population was about half native and half white. The native population was predominantly Yupik Eskimo, with some Athabascan Indian and Aleutian Eskimo. There was no special section of town for either race; the Eskimos and whites generally intermingled around the central airstrip and floatplane pond called Slopbucket Lake. Out on The Point where we lived, there were only four white families and no natives.

The natives who attended church did so in the neighboring village of Newhalen, site of the Russian Orthodox Church. The primary occupation of most of the native families was commercial fishing, although others held government administrative and support jobs with the post office and local school district. One enterprising man owned and operated an air taxi.

The white residents, on the other hand—which included most of the merchants in town—were predominantly Baptist and attended the local Baptist Church in Iliamna. Whites ran the local fuel company and the general store. All the school teachers were white and most of them lived in Iliamna, although the regional school was in Newhalen, seven miles away by road. Most of the other lodge owners only stayed for the summer and lived elsewhere in the winter.

The only government in the village at the time was a Village Council that represented the native interests. No one represented the whites. Law enforcement was conducted by the

39

Alaska State Troopers, whose nearest office was 100 miles away in King Salmon. There were no property or sales taxes—there was no local government to support.

Since the Baptists regarded playing cards, drinking, and even dancing as works of the devil, social life in the winter time in Iliamna would have been limited to potluck suppers and Bible study if it hadn't been for a small minority of government workers who were quartered half a mile out of town in a small residential area on the road to the airport. These were the Federal Aviation Administration (FAA) employees who ran the Flight Service Station and two State of Alaska airport maintenance men. A mixed bag of races and religions, they sponsored a brisk round of movies, dances, and parties to which the village was often invited.

Unfortunately, relations between the Eskimos and Baptists had degenerated into open hostility before we arrived. A Baptist schoolteacher—with more missionary zeal than good sense—had distributed Baptist literature in class, telling his native students to study it at home but warning them not to tell their parents. Of course, the parents soon found out; the teacher was transferred, but the harm was done.

Another zealous missionary had told one of his Eskimo neighbors that she had no chance of going to heaven as long as she continued to pursue the heathen Russian Orthodoxy practiced in Newhalen. Still another incident to fan the flames of distrust occurred when one of the Baptist leaders tried to convert the native mother of a very sick child by assuring her that the child had a greater chance of recovery if she joined the Baptist Church. Such stories swept across our small village like a tempest.

The natives retaliated by letting the white population know that only the natives were true residents of Iliamna and strongly suggesting that whites should clear out. One day when Mary and her mother were out picking blueberries on the tundra near the road between Iliamna and Newhalen, a pickup truck drove past carrying four or five obviously drunk natives in back. They shouted curses at them for being on native land.

We were so busy those first six months trying to get the lodge on its feet that we paid little attention to the problems of the community. Oddly enough, we'd been accepted by the Baptists as backsliders, since we'd started the girls in their Sunday School but seldom showed up for church ourselves. Not surprisingly, the Eskimos accepted us as Baptists; Iliaska Lodge had always been owned by Baptists and had even been used on several occasions as a summer Bible camp.

One evening Mary and I attended one of the parties given by the government employees. As we walked in, Bert Foss, a man of mixed native and white blood who was in charge of airport maintenance, pointed out the spiked punch—with the alcohol-free potion right alongside. To his amazement, Mary and I both took a cup of the spiked and, when the music started, we stepped right out onto the dance floor in a fast jitterbug. Everyone stopped to stare as I swung Mary around and around in one circle after another—they hadn't seen that type of dancing for quite a spell.

"You're putting on quite a show, Mary," I shouted over the din of the record player.

"No more than you, dear."

"I never imagined dancing in Iliamna when I first came here four years ago."

My first visit had been in the fall of 1973. My uncle and I had flown over from Kodiak Island in my Cessna 180 to do some exploratory trout fishing and caribou hunting. After one or two passes over the village, I'd landed the float plane in East Bay and taxied to the beach to tie up next to another float plane that was already moored to a stake driven into the gravel. While we awaited the arrival of the fuel truck—an old pickup truck with twin tanks and pumps mounted in the back—the pilot of the other plane walked up and started to untie it.

With a casual hello, I introduced myself as a visitor.

"Can you give me any advice on some of the fishing around here?"

"Find your own fishing," he said, not looking up. "I'm not in the business of guiding strangers."

"How about any places we should be careful of?" I persisted. "Any restricted areas around here?"

41

The man finished untying his mooring rope, climbed into his plane, started the engine, and roared away.

"So much for the Iliamna Friendly Pilot's Association," Uncle Bill said, walking over to stand beside me on the gravel.

"After the fuel truck gets here, let's walk over to that lodge on the point," I suggested. "They might be friendlier—and a little local knowledge would be nice before we start exploring."

Half an hour later we knocked on the front door of Iliaska Lodge and were greeted by an attractive and very pregnant woman in her mid 30s. Over a cup of fresh steaming coffee, hostess Judy Polmateer gave us several suggestions on potential fishing spots to try. "I'd have you talk to my husband Floyd but he's out flying now and won't be back till suppertime."

"You've been very helpful yourself, Ma'am," Uncle Bill said. "Can we pay you for the coffee?"

"Coffee's on the house, but if you need a place to stay, we've got lots of room."

"We're camping out this trip," I said, little realizing that this lodge was to be my future home. "Perhaps another time. It's nice to know you're here."

After managing Iliaska Lodge for a few years, Floyd and Judy built Talarik Creek Lodge a quarter mile across The Point from Iliaska Lodge. Floyd also bought an Air Taxi Certificate from another pilot in the village. He was the contractor for whom I'd worked that spring when he'd been building The Samovar Restaurant along the airstrip.

Work on the restaurant had lasted several weeks. It was a simple wood-frame structure: plywood walls and trussed roof covered with plywood and sheet aluminum. "How far apart should I space the nails, Floyd?" I asked before starting to nail down the 4'x8' sheets of corrugated roofing. A storm the previous week with winds over 60 knots had blown several sheets of aluminum siding off Talarik Creek Lodge. Such storms are not uncommon in Iliamna, we were rapidly finding out.

"Every two feet should be okay, Ted."

"Sounds a little skimpy, Floyd."

"Well, all right, nail it every 18 inches. It'll cost me extra."

"At least we won't have to come back and do it again," I said, deciding, as Floyd walked off grumbling, that I'd nail the roof down every 12 inches just for good measure. When that was done I went back and doubled the number of nails around the side walls.

The center of most of the social activity in town that summer was the bar at Iliamna Lake Lodge. The Lake Lodge opened for business in early June, when their full staff of cooks, wait-resses, bartenders, and housekeepers arrived from Anchorage. The winter caretakers, who kept the liquor store open during the off-season, moved out when the summer staff arrived.

Open seven nights a week, the bar was always full, providing a substantial percent of the daily cash flow for the lodge. Patrons included both summer visitors—contractors, fisher-men, pilots, and lodge employees—as well as local residents. The bar's main features were a pool table and juke box. Very few guests could play the old upright piano, but occasionally a small band of two or three musicians would gather there with guitars to entertain anyone tone-deaf enough to listen.

One evening a pair of visiting hunters who'd arrived in their own plane marched directly into the bar after dinner, each with a pistol strapped to his waist. Within an hour they'd joined the ever-present pool tournament, drinking and carousing with the local residents as if they'd lived in the village all their lives. In another hour, having been eliminated from the tournament, they'd staggered back to the bar for another round. A brand-new highway stop sign was hanging below the mirror at the back of the bar.

"Look at that," one of the hunters said to the other. "A high-way sign without any bullet holes in it."

"Well, I'll be God-damned," the other said. "Got to do some-thing about that right now," and taking shaky aim, he put a bullet right through the middle of the sign with his .44 Mag-num.

"By God, we took care of that," he crowed as Jim Douglas, the manager, and the bartender collared them both, running them out the door.

"You can get your guns back in the morning," Jim said, sending them reeling out into the night. "Don't come back till you sober up."

Mary and I heard the story at the breakfast table from a couple who'd moved over to our lodge for a good night's sleep.

CHAPTER 9

Running an air taxi service isn't all smooth sailing—especially when the weather turns against you. An acquaintance from Anchorage who'd arranged a fishing trip for a group of Japanese businessmen asked me to fly three of the group to Tutna Lake where they would be met by the rest of the party in another plane arriving directly from Anchorage. They were planning to fish their way down the Mulchatna River on rubber rafts, camping for four nights enroute to a prearranged pick-up point down the river. My job was to meet them at the Iliamna airport, provide overnight lodging, and then fly the three to Tutna Lake, which lies about 50 miles northwest of Iliamna.

The day was warm and clear when we took off from Iliamna, but a good stiff northwest wind was blowing whitecaps across the lake. As usual when I expected to run into turbulence along the route, I pointed out the airsick bags in the plane during my preflight briefing.

Five minutes after take-off the two guys in back were already turning pale and starting to look unhappy, while my Japanese co-pilot sat staring straight ahead, not saying a word. Another five minutes and both passengers in the rear seats lost their breakfasts—the first into his own hat, the other using one of the airsick bags. Gritting my teeth, I adjusted the air vents to their full open position with my free hand, constantly fighting the controls with the other, the airplane pitching and

45

rolling as we bucked into a stiff headwind.

Unfortunately, air sickness doesn't just go away with the loss of one's breakfast, and I knew those poor guys in back were in for a miserable time until we landed. As the plane droned on into the wind, bouncing through every air pocket, the guy on my right just kept staring ahead, as silent as if he were in a trance.

By the time we reached Tutna Lake, the turbulence had become so severe the guys in back were in wretched shape, suffering the stomach cramps and dry heaves of advanced motion sickness. But the guy in front still hadn't moved. In fact, he hadn't uttered a sound the entire flight.

We were only a hundred feet over the lake surface and descending slowly when he sat up straight, give a loud moan, and lost the entire contents of his stomach on the cabin floor in front of his seat.

I made a smooth landing despite the distraction and taxied slowly into the wind toward the shore, opening the window to help clear out the stench as soon as our decreasing airspeed allowed.

Apologetically, my passengers offered to help clean up their own mess. Using soap from their camping supplies, we managed to get rid of all but a faint trace of the smell while waiting for the other plane to arrive. The passenger in the back who'd chosen to use his hat for an airsick bag discovered after landing that it wasn't as waterproof as the manufacturer had advertised. Having held it in his lap during the flight, he decided to change all his clothes right then, rinsing out the soiled ones in the cold lake water.

Because of this and similar experiences, I wasn't particularly anxious to get into the air taxi business. But Mary and I knew that to be successful as a sportfishing lodge we had to be able to fly our own guests to the lakes and streams where they'd be fishing. We couldn't afford to depend on our competition for air transportation.

Acting on our attorney's advice, therefore, we'd submitted an application to the Alaska Transportation Commission for an air taxi certificate that would authorize us to carry passengers for hire in the Iliamna area. A commission hearing into the matter was scheduled for mid-July in Anchorage.

The purpose of the Transportation Commission in Alaska was the regulation of commercial transportation within the state, but the other two air taxi operators in Iliamna seemed to look on it as a means to control and limit their competition. They had no intention of allowing another certificate to be licensed for operation in Iliamna without a fight.

Public testimony was taken in the commission hearing room in the McKay Building on 4th Avenue in Anchorage. My attorney Bob Hartig and I arrived to find several others from Iliamna in the room: Trig Olsen, owner of Iliamna Air Taxi, along with his attorney; Floyd Polmateer, owner of Talarik Creek Air Taxi; and a representative of Wien Airlines, the commercial carrier serving Iliamna. Mr. Smith, the designated hearing officer, conducted and recorded the proceedings.

As the applicant, I was asked to testify first. Bob had me answer several questions about my background, emphasizing my experience as both a manager and a pilot before getting into the actual application for the certificate. I had applied for a limited certificate authorizing me to carry passengers and cargo for hire within a hundred mile radius of Iliamna, using float-equipped aircraft from April 15th until November 1st each season. The original application also requested a route from Iliamna to both Anchorage and Kodiak, but we dropped this part of the request at the hearing because of the overwhelming objections of Wien Airlines. I had no desire to compete in the airline industry anyway.

One of the points I emphasized during my testimony was how urgent it was for us to obtain an early ruling. The summer flying season was already half over, and there was little time left that year to make any money if the certificate was awarded.

Trig Olsen took the stand next. He strongly objected to the issuance of another certificate in the Iliamna area, citing the limited amount of business available. He argued that since his air taxi had provided all the flying for Iliaska Lodge in the past few years, his business would be severely reduced if I was to be given a certificate, thereby causing him economic hardship. He stated he was ready and had the necessary pilots and aircraft to service the needs of Iliaska Lodge.

Then Floyd Polmateer took the stand. In addition to claiming economic hardship, he testified that I lacked the required managerial and piloting skills to safely and economically operate out of Iliamna. He accused me of being a newcomer, eager to take all the business I could get without considering those who'd been there before.

Trig's testimony was to be expected; Floyd's was vitriolic and upset me greatly. These were our neighbors, people we had come to know over the past five months. When I returned to Iliamna and told Mary what had happened, she was furious.

"That miserable wretch!" she said. "And after you helped him build that restaurant this spring."

"It was probably all those extra nails I cost him," I said. "He's probably never forgiven me for that."

But Mary was bitter. "Guess we're starting to find out who our friends really are around here!" she said. "When will we hear?"

"Probably not for a month or more," I answered. "Bob said he'd keep checking for us. He's dealt with these people before. He said our chances were about 50-50."

CHAPTER 10

Our air taxi competitors may have wanted to run us out of town, but our other major competitor, Jim Douglas, manager of Iliamna Lake Lodge, realized that the more business we brought to the area, the more business for everyone. They had a full in-house staff but no aircraft for fly-out fishing and no fishing guides. Only a few days after the hearing, Jim approached me with an idea.

"Ted, we have a couple of guests who want to fly out to another stream for a day's fishing. Would you have time to take them?"

Here was a dilemma. Of course I had the time. We had only firefighters and contractors in our own lodge and we certainly needed the income—but I'd just applied for an air taxi certificate to carry only our own guests.

"Let me think about it, Jim," I said, deciding to talk it over with Mary first since it meant jeopardizing the certificate.

"We don't have many advance reservations for the rest of the season," Jim added, "but who knows? I'd sure like to be able to count on your guiding if we do get more business."

Talking it over with Mary later, we decided that the way things were going, we might not even be here next season. What good would an air taxi certificate do if we were no longer in business? So I called Jim back to set up the trip, taking the chance that the few trips I anticipated flying for the Lake Lodge would pass unnoticed in the hectic activity around Iliamna in

49

the summer. As it turned out, however, I made almost a dozen flights for Jim during August and September, most of them involving guiding as well as flying, and the increased revenue certainly helped.

But it didn't go unnoticed. We were starting to receive more inquiries for lodging and fishing as the summer progressed, so we weren't surprised when we got a call in late August from Anchorage requesting information about fly-out fishing for a man and his wife. They wanted to stay at least one night at the lodge.

A few days later, the same party called back and set up a date for the fishing trip, but this time he wasn't sure whether they'd stay overnight. He specifically asked if we'd take them anyway—a point I should have followed up. But we were desperate for business, so I let it pass.

On the appointed day, Ed Canoose and his wife Jackie arrived at the Iliamna Airport, where I picked them up. They were both dressed in city clothes, hardly prepared for a fishing trip, and when we retrieved their single piece of luggage, a fishing rod and two pairs of hipboots, I really started to wonder. Ed carried a briefcase and Jackie had a camera.

"I've heard a lot about Lower Talarik Creek," Ed said in the truck on the way to the lodge. "We'd like to fish there this afternoon, if that's all right."

"There are a lot of bears on that stream," I said. "I was out flying some photographers around the area this morning and we saw half a dozen from the air feeding on salmon in the creek. There's probably more that we didn't see."

"I don't pay bears any attention," he bragged. "Besides, I've got a gun with me."

I knew he didn't have a rifle, so it must have been some kind of handgun. "What are you carrying?" I asked.

"A .357 Magnum. I keep it in a shoulder holster," he answered, drawing out a snub-nosed revolver to show me.

"That's not much protection against a grizzly. You sure you want to go to Lower Talarik?"

"That's right," he snapped. "All this bear talk is overblown. They don't scare me a bit."

Right then I decided to stay with them. There isn't a pistol made that can stop an Alaskan Brown Bear in a charge. In fact, most modern rifles can't stop one. The average grizzly around Iliamna weighs about six to seven hundred pounds, with some going over a thousand. In a short chase, they can run faster than a caribou or moose and can tear down trees half a foot in diameter.

"I'll bring my .338 Winchester Magnum with us," I said. "That way we'll all feel better."

"That won't be necessary," Ed said. "I can take care of myself."

"I'll stay anyway, as guide." The more I heard, the less I believed he'd ever seen a bear in the wild.

After a light lunch at the lodge, we all went down to the plane. Ed took the camera and insisted on taking my picture standing next to the plane with his wife.

"No problem." By now I'd had my picture taken so many times by guests, I thought nothing of it. "Let me finish fueling first."

Ed took several shots from different angles and we boarded for the afternoon fishing trip. They'd decided not to stay overnight and were planning to return to Anchorage that evening on a charter flight.

About three that afternoon, I spotted two grizzlies about a hundred yards downstream on the tundra near the creek. Although fairly young, perhaps three or four years old, they were already close to 500 pounds.

I shouted a few times to let them know we were there.

Hearing my voice, the two got to their feet and slowly shambled away from the stream, disappearing over a low ridge a quarter of a mile away. One of the bears walked with a noticeable limp, favoring its left front leg.

"Let's move upstream," I said. I always believe in giving bears a lot of room, especially when one of them has a sore paw.

"Isn't that what you brought that big rifle for?" Ed wanted to know.

"That's only for emergencies. If we back off, we shouldn't have any problems. There's lots of fish upstream, anyway, and it puts us closer to the airplane." The truth is, I'd never come across a wounded bear before and didn't trust it one bit.

Ed wasn't a very good fisherman and only caught a few little ones, which we released. Jackie didn't fish at all but seemed to enjoy the day sitting on the bank reading.

When we returned to the lodge, Ed asked for a receipt for the flight. Since I'd stayed with them all afternoon, the fee included my services as guide. Ed objected, claiming I hadn't really done any guiding since he'd found his own fishing.

"There's a lot more to guiding than just finding fish," I snapped. "We could have had a real problem today. I'll have to report that wounded bear. I wouldn't be surprised if someone didn't put a bullet into it recently, possibly with a handgun just like yours."

"All you guys over-react out here," he interrupted. "Those two bears ran away over the ridge."

"A wounded bear is always dangerous," I said. "As for the guiding, you may have selected the creek, but I'm the one who got you there and showed you where the fish were. I even showed you how to catch them."

"We'd better get to the airport," Ed grumbled, starting out the door. "Our flight should be here in half an hour."

Ed Canoose turned out to be a private investigator hired by Floyd Polmateer at Talarik Creek Air Taxi to gather evidence to be used against me before the Commission. Thanks to the bears, it hadn't worked.

The next time Floyd tried it, I was guiding a group of three fly fishermen who were staying with us at the lodge. I'd scheduled a trip for them to fish the Gibraltar River, again using my own plane for transportation.

As I landed the 180 and taxied up to the shore, a Cessna 185 circled, landed, and taxied alongside. A man in his forties, dressed in business suit and hip boots, got out as we were putting our fishing rods together. He identified himself as an investigator for the Alaska Transportation Commission.

"Are you Ted Gerken?" he asked.

"Yes."

"Did you carry these gentlemen in your aircraft today to go fishing?"

"Yes, they're all guests at Iliaska Lodge."

After several more questions, he asked if he could inspect our records at the lodge that evening. I told him he'd be welcome to what records we had and looked forward to seeing him after dinner. Without further comment, he wished us a pleasant day and left in the other plane.

Our clients enjoyed some excellent fishing, but the morning's encounter had taken the joy out of the day for me. After dinner that evening, the investigator spent an hour or more going over our books.

"Can I give you a lift somewhere?" I asked when he was preparing to leave.

"No, thanks," he said curtly. "I borrowed a car for the evening."

The car belonged to Talarik Creek Air Taxi, but this time their machinations backfired. One of my guests happened to know one of the members of the Transportation Commission personally.

"I'll call him as soon as I get back to town," he said. "I'd like to know what's going on myself. Sounds like harassment to me."

And he did. And it was. And it stopped.

CHAPTER 11

September is undoubtedly the best month for fishing for large rainbow trout, and knowledgeable fishermen from around the world now seek us out to try their skill and luck with these marvelous sport fish. Fish weighing eight to ten pounds are commonly found swimming through the shallow creeks and rivers around Iliamna, while the occasional fifteen-pound monster is the stuff of which lifelong dreams are made. Contracting for full fly-out fishing with a guide each day, plus lodging and meals, was exactly the kind of business we were seeking.

The travel agent in Anchorage who had prepared our brochures and assured us, "Don't worry about a thing. We'll send you enough business to fill the place," was having his own problems. Most of his "hundreds of thousands" of tourists who were supposed to visit Alaska that summer had somehow managed to avoid his agency despite all the advertising he was supposed to have done. During the season he sent only four fishermen to Iliaska Lodge, and they only stayed a few days each. We were learning more and more about the business we were in—and some of the people in it.

The travel agency was to receive a 10% commission on business they sent us, but the contract allowed them to collect a 50% deposit from the traveller before the trip. We would then collect the remaining 50% directly from the client and bill the agency for the remaining 40% still owed us. Live and learn. On a trip to Anchorage in early September, I visited the travel agency to find out why we hadn't yet received the money due us, only to find a vacant office with no forwarding address.

I hope that someday, somewhere, I'll run into that man again. Five hundred dollars was a lot of money at that time, and I would sure like to talk it over with him.

By mid-August, after almost two months of fairly steady business, we found ourselves with an empty lodge. The contractor on the road construction job had completed his work for the state and moved his equipment and crew out of Iliamna. To make matters worse, with all the tundra fires out and the danger diminished substantially after the rains in late July, the BLM had also pulled its camp and crews out of Iliamna.

Although we continued to receive an occasional drop-in overnight guest and a few fishermen, business was way down and once again we started worrying about paying our bills. When school started in late August, two new teachers asked to stay at the lodge since they knew we intended to stay open all winter. Mary was a little apprehensive about having long-term tenants but Liz and Angie were excited about having their new schoolteachers living at home with them. They were both excellent students and liked school. Terry Kincaid and Gloria Behm, both in their twenties, thus joined our family as permanent guests.

Terry was the younger of the two, having just completed college and starting on her first job. A dark-haired, vivacious girl enthralled with her new assignment, she started pitching right in when Mary needed an extra hand. Gloria at 5'6" was somewhat taller than her companion but very slender. She had previously taught at Chignik Bay, another school in our Lake and Peninsula School District, and was much more reserved than Terry. Both teachers were friendly to the other, mostly male boarders but maintained their distance socially. Gloria was Angela's fifth-grade teacher and would occasionally help her with home work. Terry was the special-education teacher.

In mid-September, a contractor installing new telephone cables throughout the village asked that we provide lodging for his crew of up to six men for a month or more. We readily agreed, of course, and once again we were in the contractor-lodging business.

The day the telephone crew arrived we got a call from Phil Degnan, the manager of the Holiday Inn in Anchorage, inquiring into possible reservations for his boss. Phil called several times in the next three days, talking to both Mary and me about the lodge and the fishing. Finally reassured and satisfied, he confirmed four days of fly-out fishing for Roy Winegardner, owner of the Anchorage Holiday Inn and Executive Vice President of Holiday Inns, Inc. He was to be accompanied on this trip to Alaska by his wife Alicia. Phil emphasized the need for royal treatment and asked that we extend special courtesies toward both Roy and Alicia during their stay.

The Winegardners arrived at noon one late September day on a chartered plane. There had been dense fog all morning at Iliamna and the pilot had had to land in King Salmon and wait for the weather to clear. They'd waited two hours on the ground—after a two-hour flight in a 20-degree cabin with no heater—then had to climb back into the cold plane for the 45-minute flight to Iliamna. Alicia, in silk stockings and high heels, was shivering when she climbed down from the chartered plane, and her husband was furious at the inconvenience.

Mary had lunch ready when I returned with the new guests, but their first reaction to the lodge was less than enthusiastic. Five telephone linemen in their working clothes were lounging in the front room before returning to the job after lunch—certainly not what Roy and Alicia expected at a fishing lodge. Although everything was clean, and one table decoratively set for lunch for the new guests, the contractors' table hadn't yet been cleared. Crumbs and used coffee cups littered its surface, while magazines and books were scattered haphazardly on the sofa and armchairs. With Liz and Angie in school, Mary was trying to do it all herself.

Each lineman had carefully removed his boots before entering, and the newcomers had to shuffle around them in the entryway. Then, when we showed them to the best room in the house and it didn't have a private bath, I realized we were in trouble.

"You mean none of your rooms have private baths?" Roy asked, as if he'd never heard of such a thing. "Is there anywhere else around here that does?"

I knew I'd have to think of something fast or these people would call for the airplane to take them back to civilization and cancel the whole trip.

"We do have a cabin down near the lake," I said. "It's rather rustic, but private."

Mary was aghast. "You wouldn't put them in the Tin House," she whispered. "It doesn't have a bathroom—just an out-house."

"We'll take a look at it," Roy said, and I ushered them out the door before Mary could say anything more. As we walked across the yard, I could imagine what those people were think-ing. Poor Phil Degnan was in for a tough time of it when they got back to Anchorage.

The Tin House, as we called it, was an old, wood-frame, three-room cabin, sheathed in corrugated steel. If the roof had been round, it would have looked like a small World War II Quonset hut. I'd managed to get one coat of white paint on it that summer but it needed at least two more coats to hide the tarnish of age and neglect. The lady who'd helped Mary in the kitchen all summer had stayed there, but she'd recently moved to the village.

The small entryway, or windbreak, opened into a central room that contained a battered old sofa, kitchen sink, counter, table, and two old wooden chairs. Two small bedrooms were in the back.

Although the cabin had heat and electricity, it had no running water and past residents had used the adjacent outhouse for their nature calls. If Roy and Alicia wanted privacy, that was one place we could guarantee it. The cabin was reasonably clean when we entered, and the two of them gave it a brief inspection.

"We don't usually use this for guests," I apologized. "If you like it, we'll have it spotless by this evening."

Roy and Alicia looked at each other, sighed, and shrugged

their shoulders. "Okay, we'll take it," Roy said. "We also want to take all our meals down here. We'll only come up to the lodge to use the bathroom."

"That's fine. We'll get on it right away and move your things in after it's cleaned up. In the meantime we could get some afternoon fishing."

Roy brightened a little. "That sounds better. You up to some sport today, honey?"

"You think Phil's right about the fishing, Roy?" Alicia was not amused, although she finally did go out with Roy and me.

While I took Roy and Alicia fishing, Mary, my Uncle Bill, and his wife Cynthia who were visiting, scrubbed the Tin House spotless, scouring the walls, the floor, even the ceiling. With the beds made up and heater turned on, the old place never looked better. A linen tablecloth covered the old table, and they brought two new chairs down from the lodge. A colorful quilt from our own bed disguised the beat-up sofa.

When we returned that afternoon, Roy and Alicia went directly to the Tin House, only pausing long enough to ask what time dinner would be served.

"How about six o'clock?" Mary asked. "And would you like us to send down some ice cubes now?" She'd already stocked the cabin with mixers for drinks.

"That would be very nice," Roy said.

Mary nervously fixed an extra fine dinner that evening, knowing Roy to be quite critical of his own food service. When making the reservations, Phil had told us what had happened once when Roy was dissatisfied with the meal served him at one of his Inns.

"He turned it over and threw it on the floor," Phil said.

At six o'clock sharp, Mary called Angie and Liz into the kitchen to instruct them on how to serve dinner to the guests in the Tin House. They left shortly afterward, each carefully carrying a tray covered with a linen napkin.

The girls were gone over an hour. We started to get a little worried, when they came skipping back to the lodge with the empty plates and a twenty-dollar tip.

"They said to tell you they'd be up for breakfast," said Angie.

"And that the food was good."

Roy and Alicia took all the rest of their meals with us in the lodge but continued to stay in "their" cabin. To top it off, before their fishing trip was over, Roy had become so impressed with Mary's cooking that he offered her a consulting job to come to Anchorage and teach his own cooks how to do it right. He also took with him a beautiful twelve-pound rainbow trout for mounting—and when he heard that we were going to Anchorage ourselves the following week for Mary's birthday, he insisted we stay at the Holiday Inn as his guest.

We don't call it the Tin House any more. Now it's the Executive Suite!

CHAPTER 12

E arlier that summer, I had started converting another outbuilding on the property into a hangar for the airplane. The dilapidated and unsightly wood-frame structure had served at one time as the first official post office in Iliamna, then many years as the trading post. Later it had been remodeled into a cottage, and some of the old-timers in the village fondly recalled living there at one time or another. Since it stood on the most suitable piece of land, facing the wide driveway with access to the road and the Roadhouse Airstrip, we decided to tear it down and use the lumber to build a hangar.

It took three weeks to carefully remove each board, pull all the nails, and stack the lumber in piles of equal length. We found it to be a remarkably well-fabricated building, with double shiplap siding over the original wood frame. The two-by-fours actually measured two inches by four inches, not the nominal 1-5/8" by 3-5/8" used today. We had an enormous stack of lumber when the job was done.

All three of my sons worked with me on the project; even Mary came out to help pull nails a few times. By mid-August, we'd completely dismantled the cottage, cleared the site for the hangar, and staked out the footings; then it was time for the boys to visit their mother in Pennsylvania before returning to school.

It was tough losing them, particularly all at once. They had been an inspiration and unlimited source of energy to Mary and me all summer, eagerly pitching in to help with whatever task we assigned them. No job was too menial, and all done with a smile, almost as if they were on vacation. Their pay for the summer amounted to what each of them needed to continue their schooling during the winter: Bill back to engineering college in Fairbanks; Tom to a trade school in Tacoma, Washington to study aviation mechanics; and David to high school in West Chester, Pennsylvania.

A few days after the boys left, Mel showed up. Mel Bromgard looked like a hippie—about 25, he had long reddish-blond hair held in place with a headband. Six feet tall, lean and rangy, with a three-day growth of beard, he looked like a man who'd seen enough of the world to know what he wanted from it. He'd arrived in Iliamna a few weeks before with camping gear and kayak, planning to tour the area by water. Instead, he'd spent two uncomfortable weeks at a campsite a few miles up the lake watching one storm after another sweep through the area. Finally, discouraged, wet, and tired of the inside of his small tent, he'd returned to civilization.

Mel spotted me working outside the generator shack as he walked down the driveway toward the lodge. "Heard you were building a hangar," he said. "Need any help?"

"Sure do," I answered, "but we can't pay much. Room and board and transportation is about all."

"Room and board sounds pretty good to me right now," he said and introduced himself. "I'll take it."

A woodsman and sawmill operator by trade, Mel quickly grasped the essentials of the project. With my civil engineering background, I handled the structural design; together, we got the hangar almost complete before the first winter storm.

Mel wasn't simply a hard worker—he was tireless, and I found myself constantly challenged to keep up. On days when I had to fly or guide, Mel simply kept on at his same fast pace. If he ran out of work on the hangar, he'd come into the kitchen and give Mary a hand. His cheerful and smiling face was a pleasure to have around the lodge.

The Saturday we were ready to tilt the walls into place, we

asked all the lodge guests to pitch in and help. Mel and I had prefabricated the 16'x32' side walls and 16'x40' back wall on the floor of the building. It took both of us, plus Mary, the two schoolteachers, and four men from the telephone line crew to slide each stud wall into place, tilt it vertically, and nail down the support braces. The whole project seemed to grow by leaps and bounds.

We had only the doors to build and hang when the first real storm of an early winter passed through southwestern Alaska. The wind started picking up from the southeast at noon; in only a few hours the airport was recording velocities more than 50 knots, with higher gusts at the lodge. When Mel and I went out to check the hangar in mid-afternoon, we found it leaning ten degrees downwind, swaying slightly in the stronger gusts.

It was square when we'd erected it; now it stood in imminent danger of collapsing. Fortunately, I'd had a winch mounted on the front bumper of the truck that spring. We passed the winch cable completely around the upwind 12"x12" column holding the roof up and slowly winched the whole building back upright. We left the truck there all night and the hangar withstood the rest of the storm.

We spent the next two days installing permanent tie-downs, once again using materials found around the property. First we buried three eight-foot-long, telephone-pole-sized logs six feet deep underground in three different directions away from the building; then we attached three separate steel cables from the roof support members to the logs, tightening each securely with large turnbuckles. If that wouldn't hold the structure, nothing would.

Mel left shortly after the storm passed. After I'd built the doors, I rented a crane owned by the State of Alaska and operated by one of the airport maintenance men. With the help of some of the telephone linemen, we hoisted the doors with the crane and hung them. The whole thing cost less than $3,000 for materials and we finished it just in time. Winter was fast approaching; already ice was beginning to form on the ponds in the area, and it was time to get the plane out of the water and back on wheels.

We moved the Cessna into the new hangar in late October. It fit perfectly, with plenty of workspace on all sides. Each wing tip cleared the sidewalls by three feet, with a three-foot clearance fore and aft. So far so good: now to change from floats to wheels.

First, I installed a section of half-inch steel cable around the main centerline beam of the hangar, fastening it with cable clamps to form a loop from which to hoist the plane. Then I chained a spreader bar to the four lifting rings over the cabin of the Cessna. I hung a snatch block on the half-inch steel cable suspended directly over the aircraft, ran the truck winch cable through the snatch block, and hooked the end of it to the spreader bar.

I operated the winch, lifting the plane, while a friend and Mary steadied it with guy-ropes until it hung so that the floats were just gently touching the floor. In an hour we had them disconnected and skidded across to the corner of the building out of the way, leaving the plane hanging free with neither floats nor wheels under it.

Good old Murphy struck again. Just when the aircraft was the most vulnerable, the cable around the roof beam let go, dropping the plane flat on its belly. Fortunately, none of us was underneath when it fell. The 1600-pound airplane only fell three feet, but it made quite a thud when it hit the floor.

Airframes are put together well and perform marvelously in flight, but sudden drops on the ground can be disastrous. The frame and aluminum skin buckled upwards along the belly where it hit the floor and several rivets along the upper cabin window frames near the wing connections had sheared off. Apparently the airframe had buckled slightly from the sudden stop, just as a seesaw would crack with too great a load on each end. When I tried to close the doors, I discovered they no longer fit their frames.

Depressed and discouraged, I left the plane sitting where it lay. Here we'd just saved the hangar only to lose the airplane again. I should have known those cable clamps weren't strong enough. It was a week before I even went back to the hangar to finish the job.

Deciding it was a good time to start the beagle puppies on rabbit trailing, I ran the dogs every day for a week, listening to the baying of the hounds as I trudged after them through miles of spruce and alder thickets.

Hare and hound have played their game of hide and seek for centuries. The rabbits tend to run in circles, from a few hundred feet in diameter to a mile or more, trying to stay far enough ahead of the dogs to guarantee their safety. Fortunately, nature has determined that the hound must bark, bay, yelp, squeal and howl while it's on the trail; the closer it gets to the rabbit, the stronger the scent and the louder the noise it makes, thereby warning the rabbit of approaching doom. The fun lies in the hunter's attempt to anticipate where the rabbit will circle, and then try to intercept it. The sound of a full-blown chase is music to my ears, a symphony of the woodland, but after a week of respite with the dogs, I knew I had to get back into the hangar again.

The plane looked all right, but I knew it couldn't be flown very far and I certainly wouldn't trust its airworthiness under any but the calmest flight conditions. With no qualified mechanics in Iliamna to perform the extensive hull repairs needed, I'd have to fly it to Anchorage on a ferry permit.

The right flying conditions developed a week later as a stationary high-pressure system settled over Alaska. The wind died, but the outside air temperature dropped well below zero. Knowing these conditions don't occur very often, and don't last long when they do, I decided to take advantage of the calm air and tolerate the cold. Wearing as many clothes as I could and still handle the controls, I strapped myself into the pilot's seat.

The doors were held together with baling wire as I took off on one of the coldest flights I have ever made. Two-inch cracks around each door allowed stabbing shafts of below-zero air to howl around inside the cabin during the two-hour trip. It was one mighty cold and stiff pilot who finally stepped out on the ramp at Merrill Field in Anchorage and headed for the nearest bar.

CHAPTER 13

As our first season drew to a close and the new year approached, Mary and I looked back over our guest book and marvelled at the growing list of friends we'd made. We must have lodged most of the business travelers in our part of Alaska that year, besides the tourists and fishermen we'd seen.

Amongst the federal agencies, we took in many firefighters, smokejumpers, pilots, and bureaucrats from the Bureau of Land Management; doctors, dentists, and nurses from the U.S. Public Health Service; and social workers from the Bureau of Indian Affairs. Guests representing state agencies included Troopers, Fish and Wildlife Officers, administrators from the Department of Public Safety, biologists from the Department of Fish and Game, and a professor of biology from the University of Alaska. Others included maintenance technicians from RCA Alascom; grant administrators from the Alaska Federation of Natives; teachers, principals, construction inspectors, and administrators from the Lake and Peninsula School District; linemen and electricians from Interior Telephone Company; a writer and photographer from *Alaska Magazine*; heavy-equipment operators, laborers, and supervisors from two construction companies; plus several lawyers, engineers, land surveyors, and architects representing firms in Anchorage and Juneau.

It had been a busy year so far, and each week seemed to bring new friends—but the lodge records showed total revenues at $66,000 while our expenditures, including the down payment, exceeded $110,000. We'd used up all our savings to keep afloat so far—somehow, we'd have to increase our business revenue next year.

The first effort involved rebuilding an old cabin I'd found while caribou hunting on the Alaska Peninsula. Located in prime hunting country, it had been left abandoned for at least 20 years and had deteriorated badly from lack of attention. Its 12'x12' floor had rotted completely through. The walls were still sound, but I noticed a curious thing inside. Although the cabin was five miles from the ocean, several of the beams and joists had been made from parts of masts, spars, and oars. But I never did find out who had built the cabin. Now a large hole in the roof looked down on a rusted relic of a wood stove and half the galvanized, unpainted, corrugated steel sheets used to cover the walls and roof were badly rusted.

Bill, Tom, David, and I rebuilt the floor with a load of lumber I strapped to the floats of the Cessna and flew 130 miles to the site. On a second trip we built tables and benches, fixed the roof, and installed a new window in the open frame. I had an idea that others might enjoy the use of the cabin for hunting and be willing to pay for the privilege, providing another potential source of revenue.

To attract more sport fishermen, we placed advertisements in *Alaska Magazine* and *Field and Stream* announcing our availability for fly-out sport fishing. To save money, I wrote the ads myself rather than hire a professional to do it, but we did start to receive inquiries in response to them.

The Alaska Transportation Commission approved our application for an air taxi certificate despite all the objections of the other operators in Iliamna. Unfortunately, the owners of Talarik Creek Air Taxi were still determined to keep us from getting a certificate and filed a suit in Alaska Superior Court to overturn the ruling of the commission.

Our 16-hour-a-day schedule, week after week, had taken its toll on Mary and me, both physically and mentally. Without sufficient staff to help with all the chores, we'd rapidly exhausted ourselves. My own right arm continually ached from all the hammering, sawing, and wrenching—not to mention the flycasting on my fishing and guiding excursions.

Averaging eight to ten hours a day in the kitchen, Mary's legs had started to ache from the constant standing, and a few varicose veins had popped out along each calf. By mid-afternoon I often found her lying down on our bed, feet propped on the bedboard. To make matters worse, when we'd moved to Iliamna, I'd weighed about 175 pounds while Mary, at 5'6", had weighed about 135. By mid-summer, with my stomach almost constantly on edge, I'd started to lose weight while Mary, steadily nibbling to sample her cooking, had started to gain. By early August we were both approaching 160.

Communication between us had gone from excellent all the way to impossible at times; we'd hardly had time to sit down and talk since spring. If it hadn't been for the dump, our marriage probably wouldn't have survived.

One of my jobs was to take the trash and garbage to the dump whenever it threatened to overflow our barrels. One day I'd loaded the truck with several days' accumulation and returned to the kitchen for any last-minute trash.

"I'm heading for the dump, Mary," I told her. "Want to come along for the ride?"

"Dinner can wait," she said. "At least I'll get a chance to sit down."

We drove the seven miles to the dump and then continued along the unimproved road to the Newhalen River. It's not an easy drive, and I spent much of the time shifting gears between second and third as we negotiated the winding, steeply graded road around Bear Creek and Lover's Creek. But sunshine, blue sky, and temperatures in the 60's melted the stresses of lodge life. Mary propped her feet on the dashboard, sat back, and watched the stunted spruces, alder patches, and tundra crawl past at 15 miles an hour.

"We must do that again, Ted," she said when we returned to the lodge an hour later. "Just talking about our problems helps. I haven't been so relaxed in weeks." From then on, whenever I made the dump run, I always asked Mary if she wanted to come along.

On the first Sunday in December, the Iliamna Lake Lodge burned down. I'd taken the girls to Sunday School and passed the lodge at 9:45 that morning and saw nothing wrong. At about 10:30 I was sitting at home relaxing with a book when I happened to glance out the window to the west. A heavy black line of smoke carried by a 20-knot wind from the north nearly filled the window, blocking our normal view of Dog Island only a quarter of a mile away. The outside air temperature was below zero.

"Fire! There's a big fire someplace near here, Mary!" I called, rushing to the nearest window. "My God, it's the Lake Lodge! Get your things on. I'll get the fire extinguishers and meet you in the truck."

As we approached the fire, I could see there was little chance that anything could save the grand old building. Flames were shooting 300 feet skyward from numerous places in the roof of the two-and-a-half story log structure. Several other men were already there, standing back from the intense heat. Our puny fire extinguishers were of no use at all.

The aircraft crash truck from the state airport arrived soon after and we emptied its contents of dry chemicals on the burning lodge without apparent effect. Then the Iliamna fire truck with its 500-gallon reservoir of fresh water arrived. It too proved almost useless.

"Wait a minute," somebody called after several minutes of futile effort. "Let's try to save the manager's house with the rest of the water."

The manager's house was 50 feet east of the main lodge and separated only by a driveway and some bushes. The side facing the fire was already starting to blister. "Spray that wall, John," I said. "I'll go inside and see if there's anything worth saving." Jim Douglas and his girlfriend had been living there, but they'd gone to Anchorage.

I knew there wasn't much time; only a miracle could save the small house. With a few hundred gallons of water left in the truck, we could only delay the fire from consuming everything in its path. The manager's house was doomed. Holding my breath, I ran to the door and rushed inside.

Amazingly, there was no smoke inside the building yet and I could see clearly. Clothing, dishes, pots, and pans littered the front room, as though the occupants had left in a hurry. In the bedroom I found a few rifles, shotguns, and fishing rods, including Jim's favorite bamboo flyrod that he'd proudly shown me last summer.

Mary and two other men had followed me into the cabin and we started hauling everything portable out of the house as fast as we could. The truck had run out of water; there was no time to spare. Dumping Jim's personal belongings on top of the tables, chairs, bookcase, and cedar chest we'd hauled a hundred feet away to the east, we stood back and watched as the fire consumed the manager's house as it had the main lodge.

All that remained afterward was a large cellar hole, the stone fireplace, and a cast-iron kitchen range. Fanned by the 20-knot wind, the oxygen-rich arctic air had created such intense heat inside the building that nothing else survived. We never found out what started the blaze. A new fuel oil heater had recently been installed in the bar, but there weren't even enough ashes left to determine the cause.

Shortly after the fire, I discussed an idea with Mary that had been running through my mind for several weeks—flying cross-country, barnstormer style, from the grandeur of Alaska to the cities of the Atlantic Coast and back over the great American Southwest. Mary had never been east of Montana; most of my own relatives lived on the East Coast—two good reasons to make the trip.

"You mean fly the 180 all the way to the East Coast and back?" Mary asked when I suggested it.

"Sure," I responded. "It would save a lot on airline tickets."

"Sounds like fun to me," she agreed. "Let's go."

My cousin John Ryer was living in Fairbanks at the time, working on the pipeline out of Prudhoe Bay; he volunteered to schedule his work on the North Slope to allow time for lodge sitting. We had to keep the lodge open; John said he could even handle the cooking for the two teachers plus any other guests that might show up.

On a cold, cold day in mid-January—with the temperature at 20 below and a 15-knot wind straight out of the north—we pushed the preheated and loaded Cessna out of the hangar onto the frozen surface of Roadhouse Bay, waved goodbye to John, and took off on our own personal odyssey.

It was a marvelous five weeks. We dropped the girls off in Seattle, sending them to their grandmother in Louisiana by commercial airline. Mary and I finally enjoyed the honeymoon we'd postponed for almost a year and returned refreshed and ready for our second season in Iliamna.

CHAPTER 14

J im Coffee was the maintenance man assigned to the Iliamna Flight Service Station. He was in his mid-fifties, of average height and build, with graying hair and a ruddy complexion. One evening early in January he was driving his pickup to the airport through a light snow when, less than half a mile from home, he saw a large animal outlined in the headlights of his truck. Jim described the creature as potbellied, covered with dark hair, and about nine feet tall. Startled, it moved off down the road and into the brush, running upright on its two back legs. He claimed to have taken three or four shots at it with his .357 Magnum pistol—why, he never explained to me.

Word of a Big Man sighting spread like wildfire around the two villages of Iliamna and Newhalen, and the next day Mary and I took a ride out to the spot where Jim claimed he'd seen the creature. Since Jim was known to take a nip or two at times, I admit to being somewhat skeptical about the whole thing—but there was no harm looking. A light powdery snow had been falling at the time, so whatever he saw, it should have left tracks.

And, indeed, something had. A trail of large footprints in the fresh snow led along the edge of the road, so we got out to take a closer look. Each footprint measured 22" from toe to heel, with a width across the three toes of 12" and across the heel of 6". The stride between steps averaged 36" and the track led straight down the edge of the road.

I still figured it was probably a hoax. It would have been easy to make footprints on the flat surface of the road with a pair of plywood snowshoes. But then whatever made the tracks left the road. I could clearly see each footprint dug into the side of the snow berm, with the uphill side of the track definitely cut deeper into the hill than the downhill side. I didn't believe a man with plywood snowshoes could make such tracks on a hill. And they definitely weren't the tracks of either a brown bear or a moose, the largest animals known in this area.

Tales of Big Man sightings abounded in the native villages. One such report from the village of Kakhonak related the capture of one of these animals in a net. The creature was placed in a shed for security but managed to escape sometime during the night. Another story, this time from the villagers of Newhalen, reported that whole families of these creatures used to visit occasionally. The children were warned not to throw stones at them or bother them in any way, or they might get angry and harm the village.

These stories were all told by the older people, but the most convincing story came from Connie Wassillie, our summer cook. Connie, a white woman married to a local native, was living in a cabin next to the Roadhouse airstrip and less than half a mile through the woods from the road on which Jim Coffee had seen the creature. At about the same time Jim saw the Big Man on the road, Connie was visiting a neighbor who lived in a cabin a few hundred feet from Connie's.

About eight o'clock that evening, Connie gathered up her son James, a toddler of a year and a half, and returned to her own cabin. Her husband Andrew was out of town that night, and this is the story she related to Mary and me the following day:

The night was quite dark, with a light snow falling as Connie crossed the yard to her cabin; she said she felt as if she were being watched. With considerable relief she reached the door and latched it behind her.

She heated some water on the stove and gave the baby a bath. After he was dried off and dressed in his pajamas, she took the bath water to the entryway, intending to throw it out the door as she usually did. Opening the windbreak door, she felt as if something were watching her from out there in the dark. She smelled a powerful animal odor, rotten and nauseating, and quickly went back inside and latched both doors.

In the morning when Connie went out to the windbreak, she found the outside door open and two pies she'd left there missing. Off the step, the biggest footprints she'd ever seen led around the side of the cabin to her bedroom window, then crossed the yard toward Myrtle's house. According to Myrtle, the creature had stolen two sheets and two pillowcases from her clothes line, "probably," she said, "to bandage its wounds with, if Jim hit it."

Earlier that year I'd noticed an ad in an Anchorage newspaper announcing that Jim Repine, one of Alaska's foremost fishing authorities, was going to hold a fly-fishing clinic at one of the other lodges in Iliamna. On impulse, I'd sent Jim a letter inviting him over for coffee the next time he was in town and enclosing one of my own hand-tied trout flies.

A few weeks later Jim had come by the lodge. A solidly built six-footer about my own age—with just enough gray at the temples for distinction—Jim had the charm, grace, and gift of gab that made friends easily. He was a television personality in Anchorage at the time, with a weekly show featuring sportfishing around the state. He also wrote outdoor articles for the morning paper and already had one book to his credit on favorite Alaskan fishing spots. I thought the Big Man story might interest him so, having taken some photographs of the footprints along the road, I gave him a call.

"That's a fascinating story," Jim said. "I'd love to do a piece on it for the paper."

"I have to come up to town tomorrow to pick up our plane," I said. "I can offer you a lift back if you want one."

"That's great. Listen, I'll bring my cameraman Bill Holden along—maybe we can get some footage for a TV show. Do you think Mary could line up some interviews for us?"

"I'll ask her. Sometimes these people will talk to outsiders about things, sometimes not."

As it turned out, only Jim Coffee and John Adcox, a non-native employee of the Alaska Department of Transportation, would cooperate by participating in a taped interview. When it came to interviewing the local natives, we hit a stone wall. Connie's husband even refused to let her be interviewed on film. To a person, the local population refused to talk; even those who only a few days before had told Mary so many stories about the Big Man had now clammed up. They seemed almost protective toward the creature.

Jim took the stonewalling in stride. "I think I've got enough for a program anyway," he said. "Between Jim Coffee and you and Mary, plus the footage of the tracks as they went down over the berm, I've got enough on film to work with."

Another sighting of Big Man tracks occurred in February while Mary and I were on the East Coast. No one saw the animal itself that time, only the tracks. John Ryer and Scott Bauer set out on foot to try to follow them as far as they could. They reported that, before the trail disappeared on bare ground, they came to a steep hill surrounded by snowdrifts. The tracks never altered course but continued up the hill without breaking stride. When John and Scott tried to follow up the steep grade, they were unable to match the footprints in the snow and had to scramble up the slope on all fours, using hands and feet to make the crest. Scott said that it would have been impossible for any human to climb that hill walking upright.

Mary and I often entertain our guests with tales of Big Foot; it adds to the mystery and lore of the place. Our guests seldom take us seriously, but one gentleman, born, raised, and educated in Russia, had studied such animals while in his homeland. He said that during his own research he'd found evidence that one or two of these creatures had been captured in Russia during the 19th Century and displayed in cages by a traveling circus.

What might the Big Man be? It might be a very rare animal approaching extinction. It might be nocturnal and therefore seldom seen by man. It might be extremely shy or wary and inhabit only the most isolated and rugged terrain, as far from man as possible. Myth or fact, it remains a mystery to us—but the natives know that there's something out there in the dark, watching.

CHAPTER 15

In my humble opinion, there's nothing in the field of small business quite so humiliating as applying for a loan at a bank. On our way back from the East Coast, we'd stopped in Seattle to buy a second airplane, a 3-year-old Cessna 185 on floats. Now I needed to arrange the financing for it, so, packing all our financial records, I flew to Anchorage. I had a standing invitation to stay at Jim Repine's place whenever I went to town, but I went to the bank first.

Our balance sheet for the previous year may have had more red ink than black, but we'd managed to pay all our bills and had great expectations for the coming season. The loan officer at the bank with whom I'd done business for the past six years was naturally my first stop.

By coincidence, the officer now in charge of commercial loans in the Anchorage office had previously been the manager of the Kodiak branch. What a break. "I've got this one made," I thought to myself. We'd been friends and fellow Rotarians in Kodiak, where, only a year before, he had approved the current loan on my Cessna 180.

"Jim, I need a loan for another airplane," I started out. "Business looks so good for the coming summer we're going to need two planes to take advantage of it."

"Better bring in last year's income tax report," Jim said, handing me the necessary application forms. "We'll also need the projected revenues and expenses for 1978."

I worked for hours on our projected business accounts for the coming season, documenting why I felt we needed a second plane and how we proposed to pay for it. I was exposing my soul to an impartial jury of bankers who knew almost nothing about me or the lodge business, and it felt very uncomfortable. How could they understand our commitment to Iliaska? Did they even care? Inexperienced as I was in this field, at least I knew we had a friend in the bank to speak up for my record.

"You know, Ted, I don't make the decision on loans like this," Jim said as I submitted the paperwork late that same afternoon. "We have a loan committee that does it here in Anchorage."

"I understand, Jim. When will they meet on it?"

"Probably tomorrow."

Jim gave me the bad news two days later as he handed me a cup of coffee across his desk. "I'm sorry, Ted, but the loan committee has turned down your application."

I couldn't believe it. For six years I'd dealt exclusively with this bank, maintaining a fairly substantial balance with them. Now when I really needed help, they refused.

"Did you explain that I've borrowed money before to purchase airplanes?" I asked. "And I never missed a payment—doesn't that mean anything?" I was starting to get a little hot.

"Believe me, I explained it all to the committee," he said. "They wouldn't change their mind."

"You know, of course, that you've forever lost my business."

He nodded sadly. "I can't really blame you," he said. "I wish there was another way."

But there wasn't. They were the largest bank in Alaska at the time so I'm sure they never felt the impact, but I went directly to the nearest teller's window and closed out all our accounts, except the one loan I still had outstanding with them. If I could have paid that off on the spot, I would have.

I have since come to the conclusion that banks don't really want to lend money to new businesses. Although they're eager enough to help established firms (at prime plus 5%), entrepreneurs are too risky. Of course, if we'd been a foreign country in Central or South America in 1978, we could have asked for billions and received it regardless.

The Fedalaska Federal Credit Union came to the rescue within days. When I left Jim's bank, I went straight to their office in Anchorage and applied for the same loan. Perhaps the fact that my Coast Guard retirement check was to be deposited directly into an account with them had something to do with their granting me the loan. But once again I had to bare all our financial records for their review, humbling myself before another loan officer and committee for approval.

Meanwhile, Jim Repine had described a new company he was forming with two other partners that would specialize in the outdoors, to be called Alaska Outdoors. Jim was still filming half-hour television shows for his weekly broadcast, plus contributing sport-fishing articles for the *Daily News*, Anchorage's morning paper. Alaska Outdoors planned to publish a quarterly magazine and operate a travel agency for sport fishermen. The travel agency attracted my attention; it could send us some much needed business.

Considering our last experience with a travel agent, I was a little leery, but Jim reassured me I had no need to worry about the kind of people involved in his company. He'd vouch for them all as solid citizens, honest and straightforward in all their previous ventures. I believed him.

So, still naive in the ways of the travel business, I signed a contract to use Alaska Outdoors as a booking agent. The agreement authorized them to collect not half (as in our previous contract) but all the money from clients before they arrived at Iliamna. We would then submit a bill, from which Alaska Outdoors would subtract a 20% commission for booking the clients.

The major drawback to this arrangement was that we wouldn't receive any deposits—and we now know that it's deposit money that keeps lodges going over the winter. And 20% seemed like an awful lot of money just for arranging fishing trips, but Jim assured me that they needed it for all the advertising they planned for the summer.

"The more advertising, the better the results," Jim said. It sounded reasonable—and 80% of some business is better than

100% of nothing.

I also arranged to do some of the guiding and flying for Jim's TV show and to provide accommodations at the lodge for his crew. We were talking about the types of shows he wanted and just how Iliaska Lodge could help when I had a sudden idea.

"Jim," I asked, "have you ever fished Kodiak Island for spring steelhead?"

"No," he said. "Why?"

"There's a super run of fish in the fall. They enter the rivers on the western half of the island and winter over in fresh water. I've caught a few 15-pounders and I'm sure there are bigger ones. They take large streamer flies like the Polar Shrimp, Alaska Maryann, and several sculpin patterns."

"Are these all hold-over fish?" Jim asked.

"Many are, but I think there must be fresh runs during the winter because I've caught both dark spawners and brighter ones in the spring. Of course, they're all spawners in April and May, but some of them seem much fresher and have a lot of zip. It could make a dandy show."

"Okay, you've sold me. When do we leave?"

"First, I've got to get my new plane up here from Seattle. I'll do that in early May. We can go anytime after that. How about May 10th?"

Two days later Jim called. "Ted, I've got to stay in Anchorage until the 12th of May, but I'm free the whole next week. My partners are as excited about this as I am."

"May 12th is it then," I said. "How many people should I plan for?"

"I'm bringing Bill Holden to run the camera, plus an assistant for the audio."

"Do you have any objection to my bringing Mary along?" I asked. "She needs a vacation."

"It'll be nice to have her," Jim said. "And tell her if she'll bring along some of her cinnamon rolls, I'll do all the cooking. We'll make it a real vacation for her."

I picked the three of them up at the Kodiak City float on the 12th of May and flew the party to the Karluk River. Mary and I had arrived the day before and had already set up camp in the cabin owned by the U.S. Fish and Wildlife Service at the Portage.

Once we'd set up camp the real work was over for Mary and me. Jim did the cooking and Bill did the filming. All Mary and I had to do was catch a few fish for the camera—and the river was teeming with them. For three days, Jim, Mary, and I fished our hearts out, catching and releasing a dozen or more steelhead each day on flies. The fish averaged close to 10 pounds; the best was a 14-pound male spawner with a bright red stripe down both sides, a perfect subject for the color video-camera.

The show produced from the trip was a tremendous success, considered by many as one of the best shows Jim ever made. The relationship between Iliaska Lodge and Alaska Outdoors was off to a grand start.

When we returned to the lodge, we found awaiting us an order from the Alaska Superior Court in Anchorage throwing out the lawsuit filed by Talarik Creek Lodge against the Transportation Commission for issuing me an air taxi certificate. The court order also required our neighbors to pay all court costs, plus half our legal expenses. "That ought to make them chew nails," Mary chuckled.

Our limited advertising in *Field and Stream* magazine produced a dozen or more inquiries that spring from prospective hunters and fishermen, mainly from the Lower 48 (we call Alaska the Upper 1). I made it a point to answer all correspondence by return mail and always enclosed a lodge brochure with my letter. From these initial inquiries, we received deposits from three separate parties of two to four fishermen each for guided fly-out fishing that summer. We started to appreciate the importance of advance deposits.

The only sad note that entire spring was the disappearance of Louder. She would frequently take her remaining puppies, Scamp and Star, hunting in the rabbit thickets northeast of the village along the lakeshore. The pups were fully grown and had no trouble keeping up with their mother on the trail, but her keen nose and experience made her the leader of the pack. They sometimes stayed out for several days, returning one at a time tired and hungry. The pups usually returned first, so we didn't get too concerned when Louder failed to return the first couple of days.

When the days stretched to a week, and then another, Mary and I knew something had happened. A beagle is hardly a match for some of the wildlife of Alaska like the black bear, grizzly bear, wolf, and wolverine. Although she was a tough little dog, I suspect an encounter with one of them was probably her undoing. Fortunately, we still had her pups to keep the strain alive.

CHAPTER 16

Business developed nicely as the month of June progressed. Once again the BLM firefighters arrived, although not as many as during our first year. Fishermen started arriving in greater numbers, the result of both Alaska Outdoors and our own advertising, plus all the drop-in guests who had used Iliamna Lake Lodge in the past. It soon became apparent that we needed additional staff. We hired Connie to help Mary with the cooking again and Donna Eden, a friend of Scott Bauer, as housekeeper. Donna stayed in one of the guest rooms on the north side of the lodge while Scott was working as a carpenter in another village.

At three o'clock one morning late in June, Donna woke up to a loud crackling sound outside her window and a strange glow in the half-light of our midsummer dawn. Running to the window, she saw a roaring fire consuming the generator shack and rushed downstairs to pound on our bedroom door. "Fire! Fire! Wake up, Ted! Wake up, Mary! The generator shack is on fire!" Grabbing our robes, Mary and I raced barefoot for the door, each picking up an extinguisher on the way.

As I rounded the west side of the lodge, I saw great sheets of flame leaping 40 feet in the air from the generator shack. Fanned by a 15-knot wind directly out of the north, the fire slanted straight toward the north corner of the wooden lodge a mere 50 feet away. Worse yet, almost directly between the two buildings, a Piper Supercub owned by one of the guests was tied down for the night. Against such an inferno the extinguisher in my hand was useless; I threw it aside as Mary and I raced toward the airplane.

"Untie that wing rope," I shouted, running around the plane to get to the other tie-down. The fabric on the wingtip nearest the fire was already melting in the heat; it would burst into flames at any moment. The knots flew apart in my fingers as I freed the Cub from its tether, and we pushed the airplane across the yard to safety.

Fueled by diesel oil leaking from the generator's neoprene fuel lines that had disintegrated in the intense heat, the fire roared out of control. The copper fuel line running from the storage tank had a shut-off valve and I rushed around the blazing structure to turn it off. Steam was already rising from the tanks but chances were they could take a lot more heat before exploding. Our next most immediate problem was the lodge itself.

Yelling to Mary to call the FAA for their fire truck, I grabbed the garden hose and started spraying the wooden siding of the lodge. Since the fire had already destroyed our source of electricity, our water pump was useless. I didn't know how much water we had left in the tank—I just hoped it would last until the truck arrived.

Awakened by Donna, the guests began appearing outside asking what they could do to help. "Keep spraying this garden hose on the side of the lodge. We have to keep the wood wet or the whole thing will go," I said, handing the first man the nozzle.

When we'd built the dog kennel the summer before, we'd used the generator shack to form one of its sides. The doghouse inside the kennel abutted the burning building and was now starting to burn. I could see Star cowering against the wire fence as far from the fire as she could get, but I couldn't see Scamp anywhere. Reaching into the kennel, I grabbed Star by the collar and swung her over the fence.

"Where's Scamp?" Mary asked, running up to help.

"I don't know. I can't see him through the smoke," I said, backing away from the heat.

"Scamp!" Mary cried. "Scamp! Come here!"

Trembling with fear, Scamp came crawling out of the dog house. In her bare feet, Mary climbed up the wire fence and, reaching over, yanked the dog out.

"Where's the fire truck?" I yelled to Mary as we joined the bucket brigade formed by our guests and neighbors. "Who did you talk to?"

"Jim's out of town," she answered, handing me a bucket of water. "I talked to his replacement but they had a big party up there last night. It only broke up an hour ago."

"I hope somebody's sober enough to drive," I said, throwing water first on the lodge, then on the fuel tanks to keep the fire from spreading. The generator shack was already a total loss; we had to save the rest.

"Here it comes," Mary cried, as the truck topped the hill and headed down the gravel road toward the lodge.

The FAA fire truck is a self-contained fire-fighting vehicle that carries 500 gallons of water plus pumps, hoses, ladders, and all the other equipment needed in an emergency. Bert Foss was driving, with Jim's replacement riding on the running board. Neither was responsible for operating or maintaining the truck although both knew a little about it. We were soon to find out just how little.

The pump on the truck is operated by direct drive from the engine, with all the valves and controls mounted over the front bumper. Bert drove past the bucket brigade and made a swinging right turn into the yard to face the truck toward the fire. Unfortunately, his assistant Joel lost his grip on the rail during the turn and fell off, injuring both wrists. It would have looked like a Keystone Cops comedy except it was real; Joel was unable to help any more that night.

As we started pulling the canvas hoses out of their storage racks in the back of the truck, clouds of dust, dirt, and cobwebs filled the air. Apparently they hadn't been used recently. Bert fastened one end of the hose to the pump outlet as I raced toward the fire with the nozzle. "Okay, turn it on," I yelled, bracing myself for a surge of water. Nothing happened.

Bert opened one valve after another, trying any combination

he could think of to make the thing work. Finally figuring the system out, he opened the right set of valves and water started bulging through the flattened canvas hose. Once more I braced myself. Once more nothing happened.

Water began spouting 20 feet in the air from a dozen or more places along the hundred feet of hose as the bulge of water slowly crept its way toward me. The yard looked as if someone had turned on a sprinkler system. I was able to wet down the lodge and fuel tanks again, but by the time the water reached me, half of it had leaked into the yard; the 500 gallons in the tank soon ran out.

"Don't worry," Bert said. "Jim claimed this truck can fill its own tank. I'll run down to the lake, fill it up, and be right back."

You guessed it. About an hour later—the fire long since having burned itself out—Bert was seen heading back up the hill in the truck. He had to go back to the FAA water spigot to refill the truck.

Fortunately, the FAA wasn't running the bucket brigade, now manned by at least 25 of the staff, guests, and neighbors. The line of men, women, and children stretched from Roadhouse Bay up the boardwalk past the hangar and across the yard to the generator shack. Buckets, kitchen pots, garbage cans, and dishpans were all used and, although we lost the generator shack, we were able to save the lodge itself and all the fuel tanks.

None of us could figure out how the fire started. I'd shut down the generator before 11:00 the night before and the fire couldn't have started much before 2:30 in the morning. The lodge was electrically dead, so a short circuit couldn't have caused it.

"I don't know how you two managed to move my plane," the owner said as we sat drinking coffee in the lodge afterwards. "I had the parking brake on and tried to move it myself later. I couldn't budge it."

"I didn't even think of the brakes," I responded. "We just pushed and it moved. And thinking about it, you should have seen Mary climb the dog kennel fence and lift 25 pounds of dog out with one arm."

An Alaska state trooper arrived two days later from King

Salmon to investigate the fire. "Next time don't let it burn to the ground," he said. "There's nothing left to investigate."

CHAPTER 17

We had several foreign guests that summer, including French, Austrian, German, Canadian, Swedish, and Japanese. Sometimes their stays overlapped, and it was interesting to listen to the different accents as they tried to communicate with each other in English. Several of these foreigners were sent by Alaska Outdoors, particularly the Japanese, whom Jim Repine was courting at the time.

In mid-July Jim called to make reservations for two Japanese, Dr. Yoshi and Mr. Fujii, whom he was to guide on a three-day camping and fishing trip to be followed by four days of fishing with me at the lodge.

All went well on the campout. I'd flown the party out and back in the 185, and the two clients were enthralled with the Alaskan experience when they returned to Iliamna. Jim returned to Anchorage and the next day I took the Japanese fishermen to another of our streams, where they caught and released dozens of three- to five-pound arctic char. Late in the afternoon, I noticed that Dr. Yoshi frequently stopped fishing to return to the stream bank to rest, holding one hand across his stomach as if he were in pain.

When we returned to the lodge that evening, Dr. Yoshi went directly to his room upstairs and failed to appear for dinner. When we asked Mr. Fujii if his partner was all right, Mr. Fujii assured us, "Not to worry. Mr. Yoshi is a doctor and will be all right."

But the next morning Dr. Yoshi showed little improvement. "The doctor stays here today," reported Mr. Fujii.

"That's too bad," I said. "Would you like to stay with him or go fishing?"

"I fish. My friend stays here," he said, so I invited him to join another party of two Austrian guests who were also staying at the lodge at the time.

Dr. Yoshi was no better that evening when we returned, but after talking with him, Mr. Fujii insisted his friend would be all right. Mary and I were becoming more and more worried about him, but since he was a doctor himself, we thought he knew what he was doing. At least he hadn't gotten any worse.

Dr. Yoshi was no better the next morning, so once again he stayed in bed while I took his partner and the Austrians fishing. While we spent a fine sunny day on a beautiful rainbow trout stream, Mary wasn't so fortunate.

About mid-morning, Donna came down to the kitchen from making beds upstairs. "That poor man," she said to Mary. "He's been in the bathroom for half an hour, and I can hear him retching through the door."

"I'd better go up and see for myself," Mary decided. Preparing a tray of crackers, toast, and 7-Up, she climbed the stairs and knocked on his door. "Doctor Yoshi, are you all right?" she called.

"Oh yes, Mama-san," came a weak reply.

"I'm coming in to see. I've brought you something to settle your stomach."

"Oh no, Mama-san. I okay."

"I'm coming in," Mary repeated firmly, entering the room. The doctor lay on his bed, sweating profusely and pale as a ghost.

"You very sick," Mary said.

"Oh yes, Mama-san. I very sick."

There were no doctors in Iliamna. "You go Anchorage to doctor?"

"Oh yes, Mama-san."

"You go Anchorage with Mr. Ted? Tonight?"

"Oh yes, Mama-san. Thank you," he said, declining the tray.

"I not hungry, thank you, Mama-san."

Mary was waiting at the mooring when I landed that evening. When she told us what had happened, Mr. Fujii headed straight for the lodge while I fueled the plane for the flight to Anchorage.

Mary had supper on the table; after a quick meal, she and Mr. Fujii went upstairs to pack the doctor's belongings and get him ready for the trip, while I checked the weather to Anchorage. Fortunately, the sky was clear and calm; this being mid-July, it would be light until midnight.

Dr. Yoshi was awake and sitting on the edge of his bed when Mary entered the room. He had a pad of paper in his lap and was trying to write something in English. In a weak and shaking hand he continued writing as Mary and Mr Fujii started packing his belongings.

"Mama-san," Dr. Yoshi called. "I have something here for you."

Mary put a few last things in the duffel bag, secured the latch, and crossed the room to stand by the bed, catching the doctor's arm as he shakily got to his feet. "Please give this to the hospital in Anchorage," he said. "It is the medicine I need."

"I'll call them as soon as we get downstairs," she said. "Are you packed yet, Mr. Fujii?"

"All ready, Mama-san," he replied, heading toward the door.

"Let me help you, Doctor," Mary said, taking hold of the 40-pound duffel bag she'd just packed.

"Oh no, Mama-san," the doctor cried, crossing the room to take hold of the bag with both hands. He was so weak he could hardly stand up but pride wouldn't allow him to let Mary carry his bag downstairs.

"It's all right," Mary said. "I can carry it easily."

"Oh no, Mama-san. Not right," he replied, yanking at the bag. Seeing him so adamant, Mary let go of the bag. No sense wearing him out arguing over who carried it.

Halfway down the stairs, Dr. Yoshi collapsed. Bouncing and sliding down the rest of the steps, he landed with his duffel bag on top of him at the bottom of the stairs.

Picking him up, I carried him into the front room. "Get a

blanket, please," I asked Mary, who was standing on the stairs appalled at what had happened. "We'll have to carry him out to the airplane."

Once again the willing hands of our guests came to the rescue. Three to a side, we carried the sick man cradled in the blanket the few hundred yards down to the dock, where I carefully lifted him into the rear seat of the Cessna. Mr. Fujii climbed in next to him and wrapped an extra blanket around his friend to keep him warm.

The flight into town couldn't have been made under nicer weather conditions. Ceiling and visibility were unlimited and there was no turbulence to bounce the plane around. Nevertheless, the poor doctor sat with his head in a towel, trying to stop the dry heaves that were racking his body.

I had alerted Iliamna Flight Service of the emergency when I'd filed the flight plan, and they in turn must have passed the information to Anchorage.

"Anchorage radio," I radioed in when we were approaching the city, "this is Cessna 6527 Alpha, 30 miles southwest for Lake Hood, with a sick passenger on board."

"Cessna 27 Alpha, this is Anchorage," they answered. "An ambulance will be waiting your arrival at the dock with the medication required. Where will you be mooring?"

"Anchorage, 27 Alpha, mooring at Alaska Bush Carrier dock on Lake Hood. Estimate arrival in twenty minutes. Thanks for the help."

That was the best news I could have heard. Turning my patient over to the waiting ambulance, I once more strapped myself into the 180 and returned to Iliamna, arriving just before midnight.

Mary was waiting up for news of the patient when I returned. "I don't know, Mary," I said. "At least we got him to the hospital."

Jim Repine called the next day to report that Dr. Yoshi had started to recover and would be able to fly home to Japan in a few days. He was suffering from acute pancreatitis brought on by Jim's cooking during the campout (Jim had fried several meals with butter). The doctor had known what was wrong all along. He just didn't have the proper medication to treat himself in Iliamna.

Mary heaved a great sigh of relief. I think she'd been afraid it was her cooking.

CHAPTER 18

With both the old Cessna 180 and newer 185 to operate and business increasing, the lodge needed two pilots during the summer. The first pilot I tried lasted less than a month. Although a good carpenter—he did most of the work on rebuilding the generator shack—he was a terrible navigator and, although he held a commercial pilot's license, twice became so disoriented that, if I hadn't been along, who knows where he would have ended up? In early July I fired him and hired Reuben.

Reuben Dunagan was 31 years old, with sandy blond hair and a glint of humor in his steely blue eyes. Lightly built and almost six feet tall, he admitted he didn't know much about fishing but had always wanted to learn more. Since I hoped to use him as both a pilot and a guide, this was important.

We met in Anchorage, in response to an advertisement I'd placed in *The Times*, and on our first flight together I sensed a competence his predecessor had lacked. He was a low-time commercial pilot, having logged less than 500 hours in his logbook, but was already smoothly handling the controls of the 180 after only half an hour's flight. One more test—I had to know if he could find his way around Alaska.

"Reuben, have you ever been to Iliamna?"

"No, but I've heard about it. It's southwest of here, isn't it?"

I pulled the Kodiak sectional map out of the side pocket of the

180 and pointed to Iliamna. "If you can get me there this afternoon, you've got the job," I said.

He readily agreed, eager to start on his first professional pilot's job, and had no trouble finding Lake Clark Pass, the best air route between Anchorage and Iliamna. He had the job by suppertime.

Later in July, I got a call from one of the larger and more successful air taxi operators in Anchorage. Ace Ajax—or so I'll call him—was owner and chief pilot of the outfit and wanted us to provide complete fly-out fishing for a party of five fishermen. Two days later he called back to cancel the fly-out fishing but keeping the reservations for lodging, only now for six people. Apparently, he was planning to use Iliaska for lodging and meals but his own plane and pilot for the fly-out fishing.

This was a little upsetting. Instead of a fishing lodge, this put us back in the hotel business. "There's just one thing I won't do, Mary," I said. "I won't tell them where our fishing spots are. Let them find their own," and I passed the word to Reuben.

The Ajax party, including Jim Barrett and four friends, all from Oklahoma, arrived on the same day that our own guest, Shubell Robbins of Louisiana, arrived on a commercial flight. The Ajax party had stopped on the way to fish one of the streams flowing into Lake Clark, with no success, while I'd taken Shubell, who'd arrived in the morning, to the Newhalen River for an afternoon's fishing for trout. Shubell caught over half a dozen two- to four-pound rainbows, plus a few 16" to 18" grayling.

As I expected, Al, the Ajax pilot, tried to engage me in conversation about the local fishing spots at dinner that evening.

"Where did you say you went today, Ted?"

"Down on the Newhalen. It's too wide and deep to wade, so we keep a boat in the village."

"How about tomorrow?"

"I haven't decided yet," I said. "We'll probably look for some more rainbow trout."

"Do you have any suggestions where I should take my people?"

"Nope." I took another sip of coffee and let the word hang in the air. "Didn't Ace give you any tips?"

"Oh, sure. Just thought I'd ask," Al said, getting up from the table. The next day Mary packed us all lunches, and we went our separate ways, Shubell and I in the 180 and Jim Barrett's party with Al in the Ajax Cessna 206.

It was picture-postcard weather: bright sun, blue sky, and the air so clear that, as I climbed to altitude and headed out from Roadhouse Bay, we could see the line of glaciers etching the sides of Mt. Douglas over 70 miles away. The lake surface glistened in the morning breeze as a million two-inch wavelets caught the sun, reflecting its brilliance back at us in the cockpit.

The flight took only 15 minutes before, banking smoothly, I throttled back and allowed the floatplane to settle gently onto the smooth surface of Gibraltar Lake.

"What should I use, Ted?" Shubell asked after I had tied the plane to an alder near the lake outlet.

"Let's walk along the beach to the river and see what's happening first, Shubell," I answered, picking up my own pack and flyrod. "I like to watch the water for a few minutes."

"What do you watch for?"

"Anything and everything. Signs of movement under the water. A large fish moving to catch a smaller fish often leaves a wake on the surface. I look for insects on the water or along the banks. Right now, I'd guess, if this sunshine continues a few more hours, there'll be a caddis hatch sometime today, maybe even a stone fly hatch if we're lucky.

"I didn't know Alaska had all that much insect life—except for the irritating kind," Shubell said as we walked along the gravel shore toward the stream. "From the way you're talking, it doesn't sound too much different from the way we fish back home."

"The two major differences, Shubell, are that the trout are bigger here, and the water's colder—much colder," I said, still watching the smoothly flowing surface of the stream for any sign of life. "I don't see a thing. I think we'll have to go deep for rainbows this morning."

"What fly do you suggest, Ted?"

"Something dark and fairly big, say about a #4 sculpin or #6 muddler. There are a lot of natural sculpin in this creek, but they're bottom dwellers so I'd advise rigging up a sinking line. The black imitations work best."

Putting down his pack on the gravel, Shubell selected a #4 black maribou sculpin from his fly box and tied it to his leader. When he was ready, I showed him a good place to start fishing. "Cast straight across. Let it sink as the current carries the fly downstream but strip out more line—you don't want it to drag. When it gets to about a 45-degree angle, you'll feel it bounce along the gravel. Then start to twitch the tip of your rod up and down to make the fly look like the natural baitfish."

This was the part of guiding I enjoyed. Shubell was a competent fly-caster and, although experienced fishing with dry flies, was still a beginner fishing wet flies. The object of dry-fly fishing is to imitate an insect floating on the surface of the water, using small flies that float; wet-fly fishing, as the name implies, imitates other sources of food found below the surface. Wet flies can be either large or small depending on the size of bait you are trying to copy.

Much of the beauty of fly-fishing lies in its variety. Unlike spinning or bait-casting, where the angler does the same thing over and over again, the fly-fisherman has so much more to think about and so many more options. Flies can imitate baitfish such as the sculpin we were using that day or any other small fish that trout feed on, like salmon fry and smolt. Flies can also imitate the myriad insects from their larval stage to adult. Thousands of fly patterns have been developed, from flashy attractors to minutely detailed replicas of natural trout favorites; they range in size from a gigantic 12 inches long to microscopically small. It is a deeply rewarding sport, and most serious fishermen eventually take up the flyrod as the most challenging way to fish. Shubell was one of these. Within ten minutes he'd hooked a three-pound rainbow trout.

The morning haze had lifted from the river. Bright sun filtered through the gently moving alder trees over my head as I sat on a log watching Shubell fish. When the frantic trout cleared the water in its first explosive jump, I moved out into the current with a shout of encouragement, slowly picking my way around the larger stones embedded in the graveled creek bottom.

"Don't horse him, Shubell," I called. "This isn't your typical Lower 48 rainbow. He's strong enough to break the leader any time you try to hold too tight."

With care and dexterity, Shubell fought the fish to exhaustion, beached it, removed the barbless fly from its mouth, and released it. With a large smile he returned to the river. "I never thought I'd see a day I enjoyed so much," he said, "and it's just starting. Are you going to fish or not, Ted?"

"I'm rigging up now, Shubell. Go catch another one, I'll join you in a minute."

Shubell caught over ten fish that weighed three pounds or better that day, and many more smaller ones. The following day Reuben took him to the Iliamna River where we kept a boat tied to a tree along the riverbank near where the river flows into Lake Iliamna. The fishing improves with each mile you go upstream, and Reuben took Shubell to one of our favorite holes eight miles up river. The water in the Iliamna River isn't glacial but does originate in large snow fields at the river's headwaters. It is crystal clear with a slightly bluish tint.

Slowing the boat as he approached the hole, Reuben asked Shubell to look down into the water. Two-foot-long grey shapes were darting back and forth away from the shadow of the boat as it drifted slowly through the hole. Shubell was aghast. "Are they char?" he asked. "My God, there must be two hundred here."

"They're all char," Reuben said. "I'll pull into shore here. This is as good as it gets, Shubell. Time to go fishing."

Upon their return, Shubell was jubilant over the day's fishing, having caught and released dozens of char weighing up to seven pounds, while Jim Barrett and his group had once again had a poor day.

Late that evening, Jim asked if he could talk to me privately. "Ted, would you tell me where you took Shubell fishing today?" he asked, following me into the living room.

"The Iliamna River. We keep a boat there and take our clients a few miles upriver."

"And the first day? Where did you take him then?"

"Sorry, Jim," I smiled. "If the rest of the Anchorage outfits knew about that place, in a year or two there wouldn't be any fish left. Besides, it's reserved for fly-fishing and you're using lures."

"Okay," Jim accepted that. "But tell me, if you will, how much is Shubell paying?"

I told him. "I'll be damned! He's paying half what we are and getting twice the fishing!" Jim looked mad. "Listen, Ted, we have four more days on this trip. Could you take us fishing in your plane?"

"Sure, but aren't you committed to Ajax?"

"Not after I can get him on the telephone," he said, reaching for the phone. First thing next morning the Ajax pilot was recalled to Anchorage. We registered Jim and his friends as full fly-out guests and within an hour they were on their way to the Iliamna River with Reuben.

CHAPTER 19

September and October brought several groups of fishermen to Iliamna for the large rainbow trout, and Iliaska Lodge was at last beginning to develop a reputation for both good food and good fishing.

Jim Repine brought his Alaska Outdoors camera crew to film a show featuring the fall rainbow fishing at Lower Talarik Creek, one of my favorite spots for large rainbows. With the camera whirring constantly, Jim and I caught and released several rainbow trout of 8 to 10 pounds, but the day was crowned when Jim hooked and landed a 12-pounder.

It was a very busy time. Besides the fishing, we had advertised the availability of our caribou-hunting cabin in *The Anchorage Times* and several groups used the cabin in September and early October. Reuben and I were flying and guiding every day, while Mary, Connie, Donna, and the girls were kept busy keeping the lodge in order. The boys, who'd returned to help all summer, had had to go back to school by September first.

The last party to use our cabin that year was a couple from Chugiak, Alaska, a small town along the highway north of Anchorage. Chuck and Janet Williams (I'll call them) wanted unguided use of the cabin, assuring me that they'd lived in Alaska for several years and were familiar with survival skills and hunting in other parts of the state.

Chuck, a blond, athletically built six-footer in his mid-thirties, was physically the opposite of his delicate, slender, dark-haired wife, who stood just slightly over five feet tall. After lunch on the day they arrived, I flew the couple to the cabin, promising to pick them up in four days.

"We usually hunt from the top of that knoll behind the cabin," I told them. "Use your binoculars and wait for the caribou to come to you. They walk and feed most of the day and wander for miles in no particular pattern we've been able to figure out. You'll save yourselves a lot of walking if you're patient and sit tight up there."

"You mean the caribou will walk right up to the knoll?" Chuck asked.

"No, it's not quite that easy," I answered, beginning to wonder just how much experience Chuck really had. "Once you spot them, watch for a while to see which way they're heading, and then try to get in front of them. But don't chase them—they can walk faster than you can run over this tundra, even while feeding. If they get ahead, give that bunch up, return to the knoll, and wait for the next bunch."

"That sounds easy enough."

I could see that Chuck had never walked much on the tundra. If he had, he certainly wouldn't have said it was easy. "Just be careful, Chuck, and I'll see you Tuesday."

Our last group of fishermen for the year arrived on the same commercial flight as Chuck and Janet. Fishing was so good in the Newhalen River they would have been content to spend their entire week there, but I convinced them to try one fly-out to Lower Talarik Creek. After filming there with Jim three days before, I knew it to be full of large rainbow trout.

The morning we set out was cold and clear, with a fairly strong northwesterly breeze rippling the lakes and ponds in the area. Temperatures were slightly below freezing; the streams were still free of ice but getting colder every hour. I planned to drop the three fishermen off and return in the afternoon after picking up Chuck and Janet at noon.

All went well as we took off and headed southwest down the lake shore heading for Lower Talarik Creek, 25 miles from Iliamna. We ran into some light turbulence on the way, the wind increasing to almost twenty knots as we approached the creek.

I'd planned to land on a long narrow pond that lay next to the stream, its lower end separated from Lake Iliamna by a substantial gravel bar. I'd used it many times in the past. Unfortunately, a northwesterly wind was blowing directly across the pond.

To set down along the length of the pond, I'd be facing a crosswind; to land into the wind, I'd have to set down across the short side of the pond. Deciding to land into the wind and therefore across the pond, I realized halfway through the approach that the pond wasn't going to be nearly wide enough.

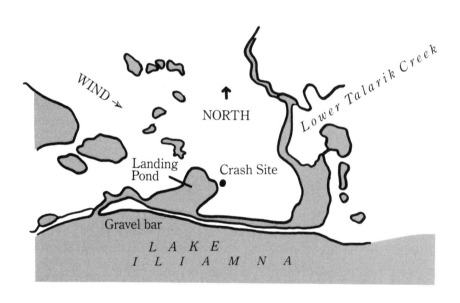

Switching to a crosswind landing at the last minute, I failed to increase power to compensate for the longer approach and, as we flew in low over the gravel bar, the floats struck the crest of the bar and we bounced into the pond.

The plane splashed heavily into the water, submerging the forward sections of the floats and tipping forward, nose down and tail high in the air, killing the engine. A harder blow and we would have flipped all the way over, but after a moment teetering on edge, the plane flopped back on its floats. Making sure the passengers were all right, I restarted the engine and taxied to the beach.

Although little damage showed, I suspected one or both of the floats may have popped a rivet or two and were starting to leak. Unloading as quickly as possible, therefore, I pointed out approximately where I knew the fish to be lying and jumped back in the 185 to taxi out for take-off. Testing the engine to make sure it would still develop full power, I decided on a crosswind take-off that would use the full length of the pond.

The plane seemed a little heavy on the water, but not abnormally so; with full power, I nursed it up onto the step, hydroplaning down the pond in preparation for lift-off. The Cessna needed 45 knots to fly; I watched the airspeed indicator creep up toward the green line as the end of the pond came nearer and nearer. With my right hand, I pulled the flap-actuating handle to 20 degrees for takeoff.

The left float broke free nicely as I pulled back on the controls, but the right one seemed to stick like glue. I rolled full-left aileron to exert more lift on the right wing and increased back pressure on the controls. The airspeed continued to climb over 45 knots when the right float finally broke free of the water just 50 feet from the end of the pond. "Must be some water in the right float," I thought, suddenly realizing the plane wasn't going to stay up for long with that heavy, off-balance weight pulling the right wing down.

It all happened so fast I didn't have time to think about being scared. The plane was only ten feet in the air over the tundra when it rolled to the right and dropped its right wing to the ground. The plane did a complete cartwheel, striking the nose, left wing, tail, and finally flipping all the way over onto its back.

The seat belt undoubtedly saved me as I rode the thing back to earth, for the door had flown open in the crash. I could have been thrown completely out of the plane, but instead was now hanging upside-down in my seat. Reaching an arm over my head, I unsnapped the seatbelt, dropped to the cockpit ceiling, and crawled away from the demolished airplane with hardly a scratch. The fuel tanks in the wings hadn't ruptured and there was no fire.

It took me ten minutes to walk back to the astounded guests who'd stood and watched the whole thing. Knowing there'd be other planes passing through the area later in the day, I reassured them that we'd be back in the lodge that evening for dinner as planned. I even encouraged them to go fishing since there wasn't much else they could do at the moment.

Within an hour our crash had been spotted, and Tim LaPorte of Iliamna Air Taxi came down shortly before noon to see if we needed any help. I chartered him on the spot to take me down to the caribou cabin to pick up our hunters and then make another trip back to the river to pick up the fishermen.

Chuck and Janet were at the cabin when we arrived—with a story to equal my own. It was midday, but Janet was inside her sleeping bag, propped up in the bunk, eating cold beans out of a can. As Chuck described their last three days' adventure, I wondered that she was still alive.

They'd climbed to the top of the knoll in back of the cabin the morning after I'd dropped them off and sat there awhile using binoculars to look for caribou. Seeing none, they'd crossed the valley to the northwest and climbed the next ridge. Again they'd used glasses but, seeing nothing, had continued along the ridge further away from the cabin. The grass was frosty that morning so they'd worn their hip boots rather than get their hiking boots wet.

By mid-afternoon they'd spotted a small band of caribou about a mile away and moved toward them, dropping their day packs to make the stalk easier. After shooting one of the caribou, they'd returned to pick up their day packs but couldn't find them.

Already tired and a little hungry, they'd been lucky to even find the dead caribou again, locating it just a little before dark. Chuck cleaned and quartered the animal and then started looking for a good place to light a fire and spend the night. It was already too late to return to the cabin.

Without making an effort to cook up some of the meat from the dead animal, they'd spent a cold and hungry night huddled near the fire and started back toward the cabin in the morning to get Chuck's large pack in which to carry the meat. Unable to find the cabin, they'd hiked all day, getting more confused and tired with each step. Once again, they'd spent the night on the tundra, finally finding the cabin half an hour before Tim and I arrived.

Janet's feet were badly blistered from three days of hiking in hip boots, but she gamely got up and limped down to the airplane. Since neither of them knew exactly where they'd been for the last three days, we didn't waste time trying to search that vast expanse of tundra for their day packs. Indeed, over the following ten years the packs have never been found.

Considering what might have happened, things turned out well enough that day. The plane was demolished but no one was injured in the crash. The weather during Chuck and Janet's hunting trip had remained pleasant enough so they could survive in the open for two nights and three days. After returning to town, Janet spent a week in the hospital to allow her feet to heal properly.

Equally important, our own list of things never to do again was growing longer. I now strictly observe the old pilot's adage, "A landing is only as good as the approach that precedes it," and we're now highly selective about who we let use the cabin without a guide.

CHAPTER 20

Octber 4th, had we only known it, was to become historic in the annals of Iliaska Lodge fly-fishing. We had one last guest in the lodge, Ken O'Kennedy from Vancouver, whose sole desire in life was to catch a rainbow trout so large that, as he said, "in the telling of it afterward, I'll never have to lie."

"Would you like to come along tomorrow?" I'd asked Mary at the dinner table the night before. "Ken wants to go to Lower Talarik Creek."

I'd introduced Mary to fly-fishing the spring we first arrived in Iliamna, starting her out on some grayling in the Newhalen River. From then on, whenever she could get away, she jumped at the chance. With only Ken and a few overnight guests in the lodge, this looked like one of those chances.

"What time do you expect to get back?" she asked. That late in the season she was the only cook.

"How about five o'clock?" I asked Ken. "The weather doesn't look too good for tomorrow—you think you'll be ready to quit a little early?"

"If we're back by five, I'll go," Mary said, clinching the deal.

The weather the next day was miserable; temperatures in the mid-30s, mixed rain and snow flurries, steady winds of 20 knots with gusts over 30. The wind-chill factor hovered in the teens.

Fly-fishing under such conditions is ridiculous—almost impossible. The physical discomfort becomes agonizing. Water

109

freezes in the guides and fly lines refuse to slide through them. Fingers refuse to perform even the simplest tasks: changing fly patterns becomes a major undertaking, renewing leaders and tippets even more difficult. Casting in a 20-knot wind is difficult enough; in near-freezing temperatures it's almost unbearable. That anyone in their right mind would submit to such conditions for the sake of an already cold fish seems absurd.

We went fishing anyway. The morning was horrible. I managed to land six small grayling, but neither Mary nor Ken touched a fish. Occasionally a gray shadow would pass up the choppy, wind-swept creek, so at least we knew they were still there. But the fish were sluggish in the cold water; even their appetites seemed turned off. Not one of our flies felt the strike of a good fish all morning.

"Stop thrashing the water," I yelled at Mary after an hour without a strike. She was still a novice at fly-fishing and hadn't yet developed a smooth delivery.

Mary didn't want to hear it and ignored me. After three hours of freezing, no fish, and me into the bargain, she called "Lunch, anybody?" Almost anything at that point was better than fishing.

The river bank offered us the only protection there was from the wind. If I was to light a fire, it would have to be there, so I started gathering the few wet pieces of driftwood I could find along the shore. Pulling some dry pieces of kindling and an oil-impregnated firestick from my pack, I set to work and soon had a smoky, sputtering blaze on which to boil some water for coffee. Mary had brought some sausage and cheese sandwiches wrapped in aluminum foil and I placed them around the fire to warm up.

Both Ken and Mary were huddled out of the wind below the bank, alternately breathing fresh air and alder smoke as wind gusts fanned the fire from all directions. We ate in silence—we'd already cursed the weather enough for one day. Mary was still chafing from my unkind remarks about her casting and sat with her back to me—I deserved it.

We lingered over a second cup of coffee, hoping for some kind of miracle to salvage what looked like a disappointing day. After lunch, we moved upstream to a spot I knew had held several large fish the week before. I knew that if the midday temperatures would warm the water just a degree or two, the big rainbows might start hitting.

With a little more forethought than I'd shown that morning, I stationed Mary on a point where the stream made a sweep around her and showed her where the fish usually were and where to cast to them.

With the wind now blowing from her left side, right-handed casting was easier. The lunch break and hot coffee had cheered her up considerably but not nearly as much as not having to cast directly into the wind any more. Within the first 15 minutes, Mary had a good strike.

The rainbow didn't leap, as a smaller fish would have; it thrashed and rolled on the surface for a few seconds until it realized it was hooked and then raced downstream. A shriek of pleasure sailed downriver to Ken and me as Mary fought to control the monster. The fish stripped a hundred yards of line on its first run and gave it back grudgingly, a foot at a time, as angler and rainbow trout matched skill against strength.

I'd heard that shriek many times before. Every time Mary hooks a fish, she shrieks, but this time she continued shrieking—tossing my own flyrod back into the brush, I raced up the bank to help her out.

"How big is it, Mary?" I called, struggling over the uneven tundra to her side.

"I don't know. It hasn't jumped yet."

"Some of the biggest ones don't jump," I said, watching her line cutting the surface 50 yards downstream. "Looks like it could go ten pounds or more."

Mary smiled, holding on grimly. "How am I doing?"

"Fine, just fine," I said. "If you didn't lose it on that first run, you probably won't lose it now."

The fight lasted 20 minutes—Mary moving up and down the shore as the fish fought to escape—and ended with a huge rainbow trout in the weeds at our feet, three hundred yards downstream from where she'd hooked it. I measured the fish at 30 inches exactly. It weighed 11 pounds. Deep-bellied and nicely marked, it was an outstanding specimen of an Iliamna Lake rainbow trout.

"We need a good rainbow for the lodge wall, Mary. Want to have it mounted?" I asked—as if there were a chance in the world she'd let me release that fish.

Later in the day I managed to hook a dandy rainbow of my own. Unlike Mary's fish, it leaped clear of the water many times, racing up and down the stream trying to escape.

"Whoooeeeee!" I cried. "Mary, look at this one!"

"Wow, that's another beauty."

"Look at it jump! Must be bigger than yours," I bragged as the fish leapt for the sixth time, racing and cartwheeling across the creek.

No two fish act the same when hooked, particularly when the water temperature drops below 40 degrees. When I finally landed my own trout, it measured 30 inches but weighed only 10 pounds

"Let's get them both mounted," Mary said. "His and hers."

"Not on your life," I said, gently releasing the gasping trout back into the stream.

CHAPTER 21

According to Mary, when I was on the East Coast attending my father's funeral, she received the following telephone call about noon.

"Hello, this is Sam Shindler (I'll call him) at the airport. Do you have any room left for tonight and tomorrow?"

"Yes, we do, sir," Mary said. "How many are in your party?"

"Just me, dear," Sam said. "I've got a ride waiting for me, so don't bother sending anyone out. I'll be there in a few minutes," and he hung up.

"One more guest for lunch, guys," Mary said, as she set another place at the table. Two telephone technicians, Randy and Paul, had been there for six days already. "He should be here soon, so I'll hold lunch up a few minutes if you don't mind."

"Any excuse to stay inside today is good news," Randy said. He was a burly six-footer, red-haired and bearded. "It must be 10 below out there."

"More like 15 below, and with the wind in the north , as it is," Mary said, "the wind chill must be close to 50 below." Hearing footsteps in the entryway, she went over to open the door.

"You must be Sam," she said to the tall, bundled-up man who entered. "My name is Mary; we spoke over the telephone. Take off your things and warm up. Lunch is almost ready. Meet Randy and Paul, also staying here tonight."

Sam, a self-confident insurance salesman from Anchorage

with a large mustache and roving brown eyes, introduced himself to the other guests, then went straight to the table when Mary called.

"You run this place all by yourself, do you?" he asked, looking around at all the empty places at the table.

"I am right now," Mary answered. "But my husband should be back in a few days."

"The thermometer is still dropping, Mary," Paul said, a small, wiry man in his mid-forties. He didn't look too happy about going back to work after lunch.

Although Roadhouse Bay was covered with ice, clouds of steam still rose from the open water of Lake Iliamna. "This is the last part of the lake to freeze," Mary said, "and it takes several weeks of this kind of weather to do it. As soon as the lake freezes all the way across, the wind dies down. It has something to do with thermal air currents. Ted could explain it better than me."

Randy and Paul left shortly after lunch. "We can't do much in this weather, but I guess we have to try," Paul said.

After clearing the table, Mary picked up one of Sam's bags. "I'm going to give you a room down here on this floor, Sam," she said. "It's too cold upstairs. Our heating system doesn't reach up there yet."

"Sounds fine to me," Sam said. "Is it worth my while to be here on the same floor as you?"

The comment caught Mary by surprise. She'd spent nights alone in the lodge with other male boarders without incident. Ignoring the advance, she walked out of the living area and started down the hall toward the far guest room. When she felt Sam's arm circle her waist and smelled the alcohol on his breath, she spun around and faced him.

"Sam, this is a lodge, not a house of ill repute," she said angrily. "My husband may not be here, but there are plenty of other people around who won't put up with that stuff. Now behave or get out!"

"No need to get so huffy," he said. "I was just joking."

"It's no joke, and I don't appreciate it," Mary said, opening a door at the end of the hall. "This is your room, towels and face cloth on the bed, bathroom down the hall."

"No private bath?" he asked.

"When you use the bathroom, lock the door. Then it's a private bath," Mary said, shutting the door and retreating across the hall to our own bedroom. Closing and latching the door, she sank onto the bed, knees shaking.

Randy and Paul were gone only a little over an hour before the weather forced them back to the warmth of the lodge. Half an hour before dinner, Paul wandered into the kitchen to chat with Mary while she and the girls prepared dinner.

"Better watch out for that new guy," he told Mary. "He's been asking if we knew any loose women in the village."

"I know," Mary said. "He's already tried it on me. But thanks for the warning anyway."

"What was that all about, Mom?" Angie asked when Paul left. She was 11 years old that year.

"That new guest fancies himself a ladies' man, girls. You'll both sleep with me tonight in the big bed."

"How come?"

"No questions now. Just do it, all right?" Mary said. "And under no conditions are either of you to stay in a room alone with him."

By 7:00 the next morning the outside air temperature had dropped to 27 below zero, wind was still out of the north at 20 knots and the wind chill was 70 below. Mary had just returned to the kitchen after waking the girls and guests when the lights flickered twice and went out. The generator had quit running.

The sun—what there is of it in late November—wouldn't even rise until after 9:30. Each guest room had a flashlight, and Mary had our large lantern in the bedroom plus the gas-operated Coleman lantern we'd used in the caribou cabin. After putting on her insulated coveralls over an extra sweater, Mary went out to the generator shack.

We'd had a power failure the week before and Mary knew what to do if it happened again. She took the butane heating torch with her and, after lighting it in the shelter of the still warm shack, she went outside to the fuel tank and started heating the copper fuel line that led from the tank to the shack. Moisture build-up freezing in the line had caused the previous

115

problem. After half an hour, her hands and feet numb with cold, she gave up on the heating. "That better be enough," she said to the frosty morning, going in to restart the generator. As the lights came back in the lodge, a cheer broke out among the guests.

"But what do I do if it quits again?" she thought as she hurried back to finish breakfast.

Mary didn't have long to wait. At 9:00 that morning the generator quit again. By reheating the fuel line she'd managed to restart the engine, but this time the generator wouldn't hold the electrical load. It ran all right without a load, but the minute she tried to throw the circuit breakers to restore power to the lodge, the engine coughed, sputtered, and died.

All three guests had left shortly after breakfast, promising to be back for dinner. The school bus had picked up the girls, leaving Mary alone at the lodge, where she worked all morning and through lunch trying to figure out why the generator wouldn't carry a load. At 2:00 in the afternoon, when Sam returned, he found Mary in the generator shack.

"I've worked on my car engine a bit," he offered, standing in the doorway of the shack. "Want me to take a look?"

Mary was desperate. The lodge hadn't had any electrical power for five hours and the furnace needed electricity to run. Outside the temperature was up to 15 below zero; inside the lodge it was down to 45 above. "I've tried everything Ted told me and nothing works," she said. "Come on in and see if you can figure it out."

By now she'd started and stopped the engine so often that the starting battery had run down and she had to use the hand crank to start it for Sam.

"You can see there's enough fuel in the filter," Mary shouted over the roar of the diesel. "But it doesn't seem to be getting into the engine."

"It sounds like a faulty fuel pump," Sam said. "Do you have a spare?"

"I don't know. What does a fuel pump look like?"

Sam traced the incoming fuel line from the filter to the engine, picked up a crescent wrench, and loosened the nut holding the fuel line to the pump. Fuel spurted out and he retightened it. "You're getting plenty of fuel, so it's got to be the pump," he said.

The machine they were working on was a two-cylinder Lister air-cooled engine-generator unit mounted on a concrete slab inside the shack. Right next to it on a second slab was another Lister, a three-cylinder model. "What about that one?" Sam asked.

"It doesn't run. We bought it last summer as a back-up. Ted's going to overhaul it."

"Maybe the engine doesn't run, but the fuel pump might work," Sam said. Detaching the fuel pump from the older model Lister, he installed it on the generator and Mary started it again. The engine ran like a dream.

"I think you'll find this fuel pump," Sam said, holding the old pump in his oily hands, "has a small hole in its diaphragm, probably caused by trying to pump fuel against a vacuum when ice clogged the line this morning. It pumped just enough fuel to run the engine without a load but couldn't pump enough to hold it up to speed with a load."

"Thank you, Sam," Mary said, sincerely grateful. "I don't know what we'd have done without electricity tonight."

"It's the least I could do," Sam said, contrite and embarrassed. "Am I forgiven? Friends?"

"Okay, Sam—friends," Mary smiled.

"But let me tell you, Mary, if I left my wife here with a lodge and two kids, and the temperature 25 below zero, she'd have been on the next plane south—and I wouldn't blame her."

CHAPTER 22

B y now we could judge guests with a more practiced eye. "Here comes another toughie," I'd say to Mary, sizing up an incoming guest as one of those who demanded everything with a smile and gave little—not even their check—with one themselves. After two years in the business, we weren't often wrong.

"Is this the best you've got?" that type would complain. "I've got a lot of work to do and need a full-sized table in my room." We moved a table up from the basement for that one.

"And there's another spoiled brat," Mary would say, spotting one of her favorites, the guest who couldn't eat a piece of toast without complaining about the butter.

"I prefer a linen napkin at dinner," that kind would insist. "I always eat a raw onion at every meal, including breakfast." So we washed the linen napkins daily that week and ordered another sack of onions.

But there was one group of guests who we could always count on to act like the ladies and gentlemen they were—those rare and wonderful anglers who fished exclusively with a flyrod. The fact that I am a fly-fisherman myself has nothing to do with it. My opinion is, of course, unbiased.

My own experience with fly-fishing started when I was eleven and my parents, knowing my fondness for angling with worms, gave me a beginner's fly-tying kit for Christmas. Progressing slowly, I taught myself a variety of techniques over the years, honing my skills with both dry and wet flies so that now, 43 years later, I am known as a fairly accomplished fly-fisherman. At least I seem to catch more than my share of fish with a flyrod when I put my mind to it.

The best parts of the lodge business for me were the times I spent with our fly-fishing guests astream and afterwards in the lodge swapping yarns. So when Mary and I sat down to formulate our long-range goals, my first priority was to take fly-fishermen only. Second, we wanted to become the best fishing lodge in Alaska, offering the finest fishing available at a reasonable price; third, we would maintain the family atmosphere we'd started with; and fourth, we'd shut down during the winter for a good rest. All fine ideals; all easier said than done.

Earlier that year, I'd received a catalog from The River Gate, a fly-fishing shop in New York State operated by Eric Leiser. I'd never met Eric but had read and enjoyed his first book, *The Complete Book of Fly Tying*. Among the many catalogues we received monthly, Eric's well-prepared and colorful one caught my eye, so I decided to write and ask if he had any advice about how to get established as an exclusive fly-fishing lodge.

Eric's answer was as prompt as it was friendly; he even offered to insert a copy of my letter and a brochure from Iliaska Lodge in all the packages of fly-tying supplies he mailed to his customers. This was to bring us several inquiries the following season.

Jim Repine and I had filmed five 15-minute television programs that summer. When he told me that Alaska Outdoors was planning an extensive promotion that winter, including appearances at several sportsman's shows throughout the Lower 48, I volunteered to help out at the West Coast shows scheduled for Los Angeles, San Francisco, and Seattle. Mary and I wanted to get away anyway, and the idea of combining business with vacation appealed to us both. I felt Alaska Outdoors would benefit from my presence in their booth, and it would also give me a chance to participate in some of the shows and learn more about the business.

The Los Angeles show was scheduled for mid-February; since I was going to be in the area anyway, I decided to try some advertising on my own. I'd gotten a listing of the fly-fishing clubs in Southern California from the regional coordinator of the Federation of Fly Fishermen, so I wrote each one a letter offering to speak at one of their meetings in late January or early February. Of the two dozen letters I sent, I received only one reply—from the Kaweah Fly Fishers in Visalia.

I planned to show the fishing tapes I'd done with Jim—and talk about the lodge, of course—but I wanted to end with something truly Alaskan. So that fall, as I sat at the tying bench we'd set up in the livingroom, tying 1500 trout and salmon flies, I memorized *The Cremation of Sam McGee* and *The Shooting of Dan McGrew* by Robert Service—while Mary, when she couldn't stand it anymore, retreated to her kitchen to bang her pots and pans around.

The Kaweah Fly Fishers in Visalia reserved space for us at their local Holiday Inn, one of those fancy ones called a Holidome, with an indoor swimming pool. It was a far cry from Iliaska Lodge. We hadn't been there five minutes before the two girls had their bathing suits on and were headed for the pool.

But if Mary and I were overawed by their Holidome, the Kaweah Fly Fishers were even more amazed at the fishing tapes I'd brought. Most of them would have gotten excited over a twelve-inch trout—and there I was catching twelve-pounders right before their eyes. I'd forgotten how good the fishing really was compared to the States. My average day's fishing in Alaska easily surpassed my best month's fishing anywhere else.

The next day we arrived in Los Angeles, and I had my first look at a sportsman's show from inside the booth. Dropping Mary and the girls off in Burbank to visit her sister Jean, I drove down the Santa Ana Freeway to the exposition hall. All I have to say about the freeway system is, I'm glad I don't live there. Give me the gravel roads of Iliamna any day. Where were all those people going, and in such a rush?

Alaska Outdoors was representing several Alaskan lodges and tour operators, but I was the only one actually present at the show. They ran several tapes of fishing on a television set in the booth and we were there to answer questions, pass out brochures, and hopefully interest potential clients in traveling north the following summer.

We talked to businessmen in suits and ties, blue-collar work-ers in coveralls, highschool kids in jeans, ladies in heels and fur coats, blacks, whites, Hispanics—just about every age, shape, and size person imaginable. I was appalled to hear that some of them still thought Alaska was covered with ice and the people lived in igloos.

I learned the first day to talk to everyone regardless of what they looked like. A long-haired young man in sandals, jeans, and a T-shirt stopped at our booth to watch the video program. Dressed as he was, he didn't look like someone who had the money to travel to Alaska for a week's fishing, but we weren't very busy at the time so I spent 20 minutes telling him about our state and Iliaska Lodge. He stayed to watch the hour-long video a second time before leaving. Two days later he returned with his father—an attorney who owned a Beechcraft Bonanza and who was flying to Alaska that summer and wanted to know more about our place.

The San Francisco show—considered the premier fly-fishing show of the West Coast—was held at the San Mateo Fair-grounds. People travel hundreds of miles every year to see samples of all the newest gadgets and equipment, and all the new places to fish.

Being there gave me a chance to size up the competition—and it was indeed imposing. Representatives from many of the lead-ing lodges of Alaska were there, plus other travel organizations like Alaska Outdoors that specialized in Alaskan as well as worldwide fishing expeditions. Iliaska looked like a small fish in a very large pond, but before the show closed, we'd actually booked two clients for a week's fly-out fishing—and fly-fisher-men at that.

When the San Francisco show closed at the end of the week, I put Mary and the girls on a flight to Louisiana to visit Mary's mother and sister Linda and boarded the next plane myself for Seattle.

The Seattle show was held in a huge arena below the Space Needle. Not quite as large in space and number of exhibits as the show in San Francisco, it was just as busy. We frequently had two to three dozen people watching our video at the same time, and I had to turn up the volume so that the people in back could hear over the noise of the crowd. One man about 50 years old watched the show on two consecutive days. On one of my leg-stretching walks around the exhibit floor, I spotted him in the booth operated by Kaufman's Fly Shop of Portland, Oregon.

"I saw you watching our show over at the Alaska Outdoors booth," I said, introducing myself. "Like it?"

"I sure do," answered Jack Moore, part owner of Kaufman's Fly Shop. He handed me his business card. "I wanted to talk to you about it, but you always seemed so busy there wasn't time."

"Let's get a cup of coffee," I said, handing him my Iliaska Lodge card.

"You're not with Alaska Outdoors?" he asked.

"We do a lot of business together, but I've got my own lodge in Iliamna."

"Now that's a place I've heard a lot about! Is the fishing really as good as they say?" he asked.

"Maybe even better," I said, steering him toward the concession stand. "You can believe those videos."

Jack and I talked for half an hour about fishing and flies. His company specialized exclusively in fly-fishing tackle and was exploring the idea of building up their fly-fishing travel business.

"Let's stay in touch, Ted," he said two days later as we were getting ready to close the show. "I want to talk to my partners about it before saying anything more."

"Fine, Jack," I said. I could feel that Jack and I were getting on too well to have our relationship end there.

CHAPTER 23

We'd been gone from Iliamna almost eight weeks when we returned early in the spring of 1979. Under Mary's tutelage, the girls had faithfully completed all their homework assignments during the trip and, to their surprise and pleasure, found themselves a week or two ahead of their classes. After two months on the road, we were all a little tired of traveling.

The first order of business was to buy another airplane. The Cessna 185 had performed well during the season just passed, but I'd found it little better than the old 180 for space. Although the cabin held six, the two rear seats were really only big enough for children and when they were occupied, there was no room left for fishing tackle, lunch, or emergency gear.

We decided the new plane should be a Cessna 206. This model has six full-sized passenger seats plus extra baggage space in the cabin. A large cargo door aft also allows easy access for carrying bulkier loads, and many of the air-taxi operators around the state had started using them.

I located a 1976 model in the Anchorage area and negotiated a price with the owner. With both floats and wheels, it came to $40,000—once again forcing me to present this humble soul before the bankers of Anchorage, hat in hand, begging for the privilege of paying them 15% interest to borrow money for the purchase. The credit union had changed its policy on making aircraft loans, but fortunately a director of Security National

Bank of Anchorage had been a guest of ours the previous summer and secured the financing for us.

Security National agreed to lend us an additional $5,000 on the aircraft so I could add a Short Take-Off and Landing (STOL) conversion to the new plane. The Robertson Aircraft Corporation in Renton, Washington advertised the alteration as a way to improve performance by increasing lift during take-offs and landings, a safety improvement to the operation of the aircraft. It looked great on paper, and I had a factory representative from Robertson fly the plane to the factory near Seattle where the work was done.

I was later to regret this decision.

Meanwhile, the fishing show I'd made with Alaska Outdoors on Kodiak Island the previous spring was now producing results. They'd sold a trip to four fishermen from Reno, Nevada to fish for steelhead with me.

My middle son Tom, now 20 years old, had completed his training as an aircraft mechanic in Tacoma, Washington at the same time the plane was ready, so he hitched a ride back home in the 206, arriving just in time to help me with the steelhead fishermen. Tall and slender, with dark hair and dark eyes like his dad, Tom was excited to be working at the lodge again. Of the five children Mary and I had brought together in Iliamna, Tom was undeniably the most interested in the business, and had already started talking about getting his pilot's license next winter. Tom and I had fished the Karluk River several times during our five years on Kodiak and we relished the idea of returning.

We left Iliamna the day before the clients were to arrive, flying directly to the same cabin on the Karluk that Jim Repine and I had used the year before. It was a mess—garbage and litter covered the floor and surrounding area outside—so Tom and I spent two hours cleaning the place up, bagging all the unburnable trash in plastic sacks that we loaded into the 206 for disposal in town. It was a full 206 load, evidence that no one had bothered to do it since our last visit.

I picked up our clients at the Kodiak City Dock: Don Baldwin, the organizer of the party who owned a casino and several grocery stores in Reno, had brought the group to Alaska in his private airplane; Bob Murphy was the head football coach at the University of California, Santa Cruz campus; Bob McDonald was an attorney in Reno and was chairman of the Nevada State Fish and Game Board; and Don Manoukian, currently a Reno real estate developer, had been a professional football player and professional wrestler until age forced him into a more sedentary life. Don Baldwin's professional pilot, Lloyd Hill, was the fifth member of the group.

Don Baldwin was the best fisherman of the lot and handled a flyrod like a pro. He caught at least five or six steelhead each day, several over ten pounds, carefully releasing each back into the frigid stream. Bob Murphy and Don Manoukian were average fishermen who alternately used spinning rods and flyrods. They caught a few fish but had a better time joshing each other and everyone else in the group. Lloyd seldom fished; he took pleasure in reading and sharing flying stories with me in the evening.

Bob McDonald was a beginner with a flyrod; although not lacking in enthusiasm, his inexperience soon became evident. He managed to land some smaller fish but was never able to hook and hold a big one. By the end of the week, I was hard pressed to find a fish so eager to be caught it would jump onto his ill-cast fly.

On the next to last day of the trip, I loaded the party into the plane and took them to the Fraser River, another steelhead stream 10 minutes by air from the Karluk. We landed in Fraser Lake and walked a mile down a dirt road to the falls. The Alaska Department of Fish and Game had constructed a fish ladder around the falls to allow migrating salmon to get to the spawning gravel beds at the headwaters of the river system. It was a seasonal operation and not yet in service. We fished the river below the falls, where Tom stayed to help Bob locate fish and try to catch them while I took the other three fishermen downstream.

We were only a few hundred feet away when Bob started whooping and hollering. He had finally hooked a beauty, as big as any we'd landed all week. The fight was on.

Everyone quit fishing to watch the battle. The steelhead leaped clear of the water several times in an explosive effort to dislodge the fly solidly imbedded in its jaw, racing downstream past us in a surge of strength. As Bob started to work the fish back upstream, the group gathered at his elbow to give advice.

"More line," Don yelled. "Give him more line when he pulls like that or you'll lose him."

"Take in the slack!" I shouted as the fish rolled toward us.

"Reel in or he'll get away," Don cried. He'd already landed enough of these fighters to know their tricks. "Run backwards up the bank if you have to."

"Watch that tree," Tom warned as the fish streaked toward the bank. The roots hung down into the water under the bank.

"He's into my backing and still running," Bob shouted. "What should I do?"

"Run! Run! Run!" everyone shouted.

The first frenzied minutes of a fight with a steelhead on light tackle can be hectic. Bob ran up and down the gravel bar as the fish surged back and forth across the river trying to follow half a dozen different directions at once. He finally eased the huge trout out of the river onto the grassy bank, and I quickly took a measurement with my hands. The fish was an inch shorter than four of my nine-inch spans.

"Thirty-five inches, Bob," I said. "If you ever wanted to have one mounted, you couldn't do better than this one."

"No, I want to release him," Bob answered proudly. "How much do you think it weighs?"

"He's pretty hefty," I said, weighing the fish in my hands. "A good 15 pounds I'd say."

The fish, a sleek male in full spawning colors, had a broad red stripe running down each side and a huge mouth. "Let's take plenty of pictures," Bob said. "Then let him go."

The fish recovered quickly in the cold water and slowly swam out of my supporting hands. Bob watched it go with a smile.

"Thanks for letting it go," I said, climbing back up onto the bank. "We need fish that size to spawn the next generation."

"How much did you say it weighed?" Bob asked.

"About 15 pounds," I repeated

Bob looked me right in the eye. "It'll be at least 17 by the time I get back to Reno."

Of such experiences are fish stories made. Indeed, the fish had already grown to 17 pounds by supper, and who knows how large it is now.

Mary Gerken

Angela and Elizabeth with Louder's first puppies, 1977.

Iliaska Lodge, 1978

Generator house fire, 3:00 a.m., June 1978. Note the singed wingtip on the airplane in the foreground.

Cessna 180 N6527A -- our first aircraft, 1977.

Hangar construction, 1977

The caribou hunting cabin

Chapter 24

For the first time, we looked forward to our opening week, for this year we had a few guest reservations. Two gentlemen from Idaho had reserved space and my contact with Jack Moore at the Seattle sports show had finally produced results when a representative of Kaufmann's Fly Shop telephoned to ask about rates, brochures, and openings for the season. Since no one from Kaufmann's had ever seen Iliamna, I invited one or two to come up "on the house" for a first-hand view. The next day I got another call: Randall Kaufmann and Jack Moore would like to see for themselves if all the stories about Iliamna fishing were true.

On June 7th, Randall, Jack, and the two from Idaho arrived to start the new season. Randall, a tall, rangy, dark-haired man in his early '30s, was a personable and entertaining guest, extremely knowledgeable about flies and fly-fishing, and the author of *Nymphs*, a book about fly-fishing with the larva and pupa stages of aquatic insects. He was also an accomplished photographer and took dozens of rolls of film during the four days they were able to stay with us. On opening day I took Randall and Jack to the mouth of the Branch River for rainbow trout, while Reuben, flying the old 180 again, took the two men from Idaho to the Brooks River for rainbows.

The cover photo for Kaufmann's Fly Shop 1980 Catalog was taken by Randall on our first day's fishing: a marvelous shot of Jack cradling a colorful seven-pound rainbow trout with the lake and snow-capped mountains in the background. Before they left, Randall and I had agreed to have Kaufmann's send fly-fishermen to Iliaska.

By the middle of June, we were averaging four to six fishermen a week. Although the majority were still fishermen who used spinners, more and more fly-fishermen were starting to notice us and fill some of the empty days on our calendar. Among these were two coal miners from Pennsylvania who'd saved their money for several years just to make the trip north.

After seven days of fishing, these two blue-collar fishermen were overawed by the numbers and size of fish they'd seen and caught. Stanley, the older of the two, who was married and foreman in his plant, had no doubts about having to return to Pittsburgh, but Bill was a bachelor and had other ideas.

"Ted, do you ever hire guides?" Bill asked. "Or do you and Reuben do it all yourselves?"

"I've thought about it, Bill," I said, "but so far we haven't had enough business to pay for them. And my sons guide a little."

"As a favor, would you think about it now?" Bill asked. "I want to apply for a job."

I thought he was joking and laughed. "Hey, I'm serious," he said. "I'd be perfectly willing to leave mining for the rest of the summer—maybe the rest of my life—for a chance to work here."

"There's more to it than fishing, you know."

"I'll do anything—haul garbage, dig ditches, wash dishes, you name it. What do you think you could pay for a handyman?"

"Not much, I'm afraid. We're really just getting started ourselves," I said. "With what we can afford, you might not even have enough to get back to Pittsburgh."

"I've already got my ticket back," he said. "What do you say?"

"I'll talk to Mary about it, but don't get your hopes up, Bill," I said. "We're barely holding our own now; maybe in a few years."

The day the miners left we greeted Jim McBride and Craig Leonard, two fly-fishing dentists from Long Beach, California. Craig, the taller of the two, was in his forties, dark-haired and slender, with a constant twinkle in his eye. Jim was shorter, stouter, and wore glasses. They were above-average fly-fishermen and a little competitive with each other in a friendly way.

They fished at our usual spots for trout, char, and grayling, doing well at each place. Halfway through the week I suggested a change of pace.

"There's a good run of kings in the Nushagak River this year," I said. "Interested in trying your luck on salmon?"

Jim and Craig looked at each other, shrugged, and nodded. "Why not?" Craig said. "I don't know how you're going to top the last three days, but we're willing to try. Right Jim?"

"You bet. When do we go?"

We boarded the 206 the next morning and headed west to try our luck on those largest of Pacific salmon. The average fish weighs 25 to 30 pounds, with an occasional monster of 50 to 60. On a flyrod they create the ultimate test of tackle, for few of these larger monsters has ever been landed from shore without the aid of a boat. Even the 25-pounders give a magnificent fight from the beach, requiring patience, talent, and a strong leader.

A plane could land almost anywhere along the lower stretches of the Nushagak. From the air I'd seen fish working along the shore line and suspected they were salmon, so I landed and beached the plane on a gravel bar at the end of an island on the east side of the river. As we moored the airplane, dozens of arctic terns wheeled and dove at us, emitting a piercing *keer-keer-keer* as if to say, "We were here first, get off our island!"

The island was a half-mile-long overgrown gravel and sand bar that had been formed by the river in past floods; now it was sparsely covered by willows, smaller shrubs, and grasses. The resident terns, smaller members of the gull family with sharply pointed wings and two long tail feathers, had chosen the island as a nesting area. The gray and white, black-capped birds laid their eggs in the grassy areas, scooping out a shallow depression in the gravel to hold their eggs.

The aerobatic prowess of these birds is phenomenal; we've often watched them at the lodge, where there's a large colony nesting on an island only a few hundred yards from our dining room window. We've often seen them drive away the hawks and bald eagles that live around Iliamna. When one of these larger predators approaches the island, the terns rise as a cloud to intercept. Swift and agile in the air, they attack from the side, above, and below, streaking in to peck at all parts of the larger bird until it retreats to seek a safer meal elsewhere. Only the raven has the temperament and determination to withstand a concentrated attack by arctic terns.

To escape the terns, we waded a few feet out into the water and started fishing, the terns settling back on their nests to leave us alone as long as we stayed off their island. Every now and then, when one of us returned to the beach, the birds rose as a horde to intercept and drive away the invader. None of us dared venture far without a hat; I've seen terns strike humans on the head with their bills, occasionally drawing blood. They also can hover in mid-air like a hummingbird.

Jim was so enamored by these aerial dive bombers that he asked his buddy Craig to try and get a picture of one poised directly over his head. Putting his rod down, Jim walked only a few feet toward the center of the island when a dozen angry terns launched to the attack, one bird hovering directly over his head, shrieking insults.

"That's great," called Craig, focusing the camera. "Take your hat off, it's casting a shadow on your face." Jim swept away his hat with a big smile.

The tern had only been waiting. Swooping down, it let fly two feet over Jim's head, making a direct hit before climbing back to a safe altitude ten feet in the air.

"I got it!" shouted Craig triumphantly, clicking the shutter just as a large white sticky blob struck Jim's forehead, ran down the bridge of his nose, and splattered both sides of his glasses.

CHAPTER 25

At first, the significance of sockeye salmon to Iliamna sport fishing escaped me. Mary and I were so concerned with developing a business that we had little time to worry about outside problems.

The biologists working for the Alaska Department of Fish and Game hadn't expected the sockeye salmon run of 1979 to be a particularly large one, but three factors had an impact on the escapement that year. 'Escapement' is the term used for the number of salmon that 'escape' the nets of commercial fishermen in Bristol Bay and make their way up the numerous rivers and streams to spawn. Usually the commercial fishermen harvest 50% of each year's return, after which the fish have to face such freshwater hazards as bears, seals, otters, eagles, seagulls, subsistence fishermen, and sport fishermen.

The sockeye salmon lives four or five years, the first two in fresh water where it grows to three or four inches long. These little smolt then migrate to the sea, where they grow to five to seven pounds feeding on plankton. During the first two years in the lives of the 1979 spawners, weather and stream conditions in southwestern Alaska had been excellent, and tens of millions of smolt had entered the sea.

Perhaps equally significant, in 1976 the United States Congress passed the Magnuson Fishery Conservation and Management Act that extended the control of fishing rights to 200 miles off our coasts. For several years the U.S. Government, through various treaties and agreements with foreign governments, particularly the Japanese, had worked toward restricting the harvest of our salmon stocks on the high seas. The Magnuson Act was an enforcement club designed to force other nations to adopt a more conservative fishing management program.

Even more important, a strike by the commercial salmon fisher-men in Bristol Bay over the price paid to them by the canneries shut down the industry for eight days during the height of the run, and millions of salmon escaped upriver. Over eleven million entered Lake Iliamna that season, turning our rivers red with spawners. The entire ecosystem benefitted—bears, seals, otters, eagles, seagulls, and, of course, us.

Not only were there salmon, but the rainbow trout, char and grayling go on a feeding rampage when there's a large salmon run, consuming large amounts of salmon eggs and dead fish in the summer as well as fry and smolt the following spring. They conse-quently grow to the large sizes that attract that most benevolent of predators, the fly-fisherman.

Sport fishing for the next year or two was expected to be excellent. More immediately, as word spread around Anchorage of the salmon run, fishermen flocked to the area, bringing us lots of business.

Alaska Outdoors was also pushing their advertising among the tourists in Anchorage and sending us a substantial number of clients. The lodge was busier with fishermen than it had been at any time in the past two years, providentially since we no longer had any contractors or firefighters to fill in the gaps. Once again we were able to start setting money aside for the coming winter.

Jim Repine and his Alaska Outdoors crew filmed four more shows with us that summer, one on sockeye salmon using light flyrods, another on Northern pike using bass bugs, a third on grayling with dry flies, and a fourth with the beagles on Rabbit Island, chasing arctic hare. The salmon fishing show turned out to be the best of the year; it started with a telephone conversation.

"Evan Swensen calling, Ted. How are you fixed for space this week?"

"Lots of room, Evan," I said. "What's up?"

"We've run into a small problem," Evan said. "Dave Engebretson, the Western editor of *Fly Fishing Magazine*, is in town. We were going to take him to Unalakleet to fish for silver salmon but the river's flooding over its banks. Could we send him down to you for a few days?"

"Okay, Evan," I said. "Are you planning to use him in the filming?"

"That's right," Evan said. "He'll be a visiting sports personality in the shows. And speaking of that, Jim won't be able to make it to the lodge until Thursday. We're going to use Hunter Fisher, the taxidermist, to act as host for the Wednesday filming."

This was a change. Jim had done all the shows himself in the past. "How large a staff will there be this time, Evan?"

"Bill Holden will come down with Jim on Thursday," Evan said. "We're going to use his assistant, Dave Merwin, on the camera Wednesday. Can you provide someone to handle the sound for us?

"One of the boys can do it, I guess. Anything else?"

"Just one more thing. We've hired Jim's daughter Cathy to work for us in publicity. He wants to bring her along to help with the show and see your lodge."

I added the totals in my head. "That makes three for Wednesday night and three more on Thursday, right?" I asked. "That's a lot of people. How many shows do you plan to shoot?"

"As many as you have time for. We need 13 more segments before the summer's over," he answered. "Everyone has to be back here by Monday."

Dave Engebretson, a tall, ruggedly handsome outdoorsman from Idaho, arrived the next day. His charming smile and friendly personality soon had us all enjoying his company, and we could see the benefit of having him in our video programs. I took him fishing for three days with some of the other guests while we waited for the film crew to arrive.

Hunter Fisher had been in the taxidermy business for many years in Anchorage and, with a partner, owned Hunter Fisher Taxidermy. His 60 years, most of them in Alaska, had weathered his face to a craggy map of smiles. He and the cameraman arrived on the Wien Airlines evening flight, just in time for dinner.

"What do you have cooked up for us tomorrow, Ted?" Hunter asked. "Jim said something about dry-fly fishing for grayling."

"The Kijik River is the perfect place for grayling," I said. "I was up there last week and the river was teeming with them, some up to 20 inches. They were taking dry flies in water only a foot deep, and the stream is so clear you can see most of the fish you cast to. It's a setup."

"I didn't know there was any dry-fly fishing in Alaska," Dave said. "Fortunately, I brought a few with me just in case," and opened a box containing at least 24 dozen dry flies.

"Lucky you," Hunter grumbled. He was a wet-fly fisherman.

The next day turned warm and sunny, with a light breeze rippling the waters of Roadhouse Bay as Hunter, Dave, and I boarded the 206. The camera had been set up on the pier and continued rolling as we taxied out and took off. Two minutes later, cameraman Dave Merwin recorded our arrival back at Iliamna as I landed, taxied in, and beached the plane. We did the same thing half an hour later at Kijik Lake, landing first to unload the camera, then taking off again to circle and land so he could film it.

Kijik Lake lies in a narrow valley a few miles west of Lake Clark. The mountain to the west is bare of vegetation and streaked by the trails of caribou, moose, sheep, and bear along its ore-laden slopes. Red, orange, and yellow hues marked the steeply-sided talus slides, bright against the blue sky above and green spruces below. Again with the camera rolling, we assembled our lightest flyrods and set off down the stream toward where I'd seen the grayling. In such a beautiful setting, what could go wrong?

The second I saw the river, I knew I was in trouble. Instead of grayling, all I could see were sockeye salmon—hundreds of them, in every hole, riffle, and run. The bodies of half the fish had already turned fiery red and the heads a bright green in preparation for spawning. The other half ranged from the silver of ocean fish to pink, depending on how long each had been in fresh water.

"Where are the grayling, Ted?" Hunter asked.

"Never mind the grayling!" Dave shouted, his rod already curving in a tight arc as he hooked his first salmon. "Waaahooooooo! You'll never get a fight like this out of a grayling. Take those dry flies off and try a wet."

The show turned out to be a winner. With Dave Merwin on camera, Dave Gerken on sound, and Dave Engebretson, Hunter, and me on the flyrod, we caught 30 salmon in two hours, keeping two of the fresh ones for dinner and releasing the rest.

"This is the best dry-fly fishing I've ever seen," Hunter joked. "You found any grayling yet, Ted?"

CHAPTER 26

A party of five fishermen arrived in August to combine some fly-out fishing with a short overnight raft trip down one of our rivers. We provided the rafts, tent, and food for the float trip and they brought everything else.

They were all about the same age—late twenties to early thirties—and came from Colorado: Brad and Kathy Stevens from Denver, Steve Parrish from Cheyenne, Rick Ellison from Boulder, and Steve Conrad from Arvada. The weather for the first two days of their stay was pleasant, with plenty of sunshine, light winds, and temperatures in the high 60s. Unfortunately, a storm that had moved up the Aleutian chain arrived the morning they were to start rafting, bringing wind, rain, and temperatures down to the mid-40s.

"It's going to be a little rough out there for a few days," I said at breakfast. "Are you sure you want to try it?"

"What's it likely to be doing on the Gibraltar River?" Rick asked.

"If it's blowing 25 knots here, it's usually 35 over there."

Kathy looked doubtful. "That can be pretty nasty in the rain, Rick," she said.

"And tough to fly-fish in," Brad added. They were all fly-fishermen.

"I'm game to try it," Rick said. "What about you others?"

Both Steves agreed to go along if the rest would. Having come this far, they decided to try it and hope the storm passed quickly.

141

"I'll take two of you and most of the gear over on the first flight," I said. Rick and Steve Parrish quickly volunteered. "Get your stuff together and meet me at the airplane in 30 minutes."

"How long will it take?" Steve Conrad wanted to know.

"Usually only 15 minutes. In this wind, about 20."

With the rafts, a brand-new tent we'd purchased that spring just for this trip, and Rick and Steve and their personal gear, I took off from Roadhouse Bay in a 25-knot wind. It had increased to 30 by the time we reached Gibraltar Lake and I dropped them off in the lee of a cove on its northeast side. Delivering the remaining three an hour later, I wished them a pleasant trip and promised to pick them up at the other end of the Gibraltar River in three days.

The storm didn't abate overnight; in fact, it increased in intensity as the days passed so that, by the time I was supposed to pick them up, it was blowing a gale across the lake. Intending to land only if I could do so safely, I took off from the protected bay behind the lodge and flew out over Lake Iliamna. Looking down from my plane, I could see row on row of eight- to- ten-foot waves rolling across the surface of the lake, the 35 knot wind whipping spray from each foam-flecked crest. "If the engine should fail today," I thought, "floats or not, nothing could survive in that maelstrom."

The river ran through a series of low hills until, about 50 yards from Lake Iliamna, it turned abruptly to the right and ran parallel to the lake for 300 yards before jogging to the left and flowing into the lake. As I circled overhead, I saw all five of them huddled under one of the still-inflated rafts on the beach. They stood up to wave as the plane passed overhead, looking so wet and cold and miserable that I decided to land despite the choppy look of the lake below.

My airspeed on touchdown was a normal 45 knots, but the headwind over the water was so strong, my speed dropped to a mere 15, meaning the actual wind velocity was about 30 knots. While my landing was fairly gentle, taking off again wouldn't be quite so smooth, although not dangerous. The biggest problem was trying to taxi the plane across the swells on the lake. The wind was blowing at an angle across the dog-leg of the river.

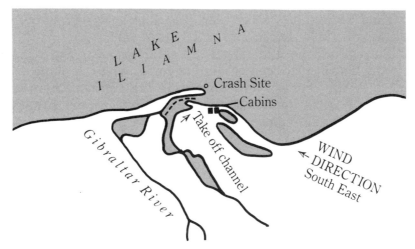

Somehow I had to navigate the plane into the river mouth using the water rudders and engine power to counteract the wind pushing against the tail. It took me at least 15 minutes to coax the plane into the mouth of the river and beach it near the five rafters.

"By God, are we glad to see you," Brad said as I jumped out and grabbed one of the float ropes to hold the plane against the beach.

"Grab hold of this line and hang on," I yelled as the plane surged backwards toward the open water. "Rick, grab hold of the other float."

They could see that action, not conversation, was needed, and all five campers rushed to lend a hand holding onto the plane. "I'll take three of you out first, with one of the rafts," I said. "The other two will have to wait for the next trip."

With the channel running generally east and west and the wind from the southeast, I decided to take off on the river itself rather than out on the choppy lake. With 300 hundred yards of fairly smooth water, it looked like the easiest and softest runway.

"Who wants to go first?" I asked.

"We'll go," Brad and Kathy answered together.

"Does weight matter, Ted?" Steve Conrad asked.

"It usually does, but you three are all about the same size."

"Then I might as well go now, if Rick and Steve don't mind waiting a little longer in this gale," Steve said.

"Okay, you three climb aboard," I said. "Rick and Steve, hold onto the floats until I can get in. I'm going to let the plane drift back into the channel and then start the engine. This wind should drift us backwards up the channel until we get to the dog leg, even with the engine running. We'll take off from there." The engine was still warm from the flight over, so, with a quick glance at my instruments after the plane had drifted into position, I pushed the throttle forward all the way. The airplane fairly leaped ahead, the strong wind giving extra lift to the wings, and we were airborne in less than a hundred yards. Although we bounced around a little in the turbulent air, we were back at the lodge ten minutes later.

If anything, the wind was even stronger on the second trip, whipping spray off the tops of the waves as I landed at the pickup point. Once again it took me 15 minutes or more to maneuver the plane into the mouth of the river and beach it near the pile of camping gear on the shore. The wind was blowing in gusts and had veered another 20 degrees off the beach, creating more of a crosswind for the next take-off.

"First man take the co-pilot's seat," I ordered, after we'd finished loading all the remaining gear. Rick jumped onto the left float and climbed into the cabin of the plane.

"I'll try to hold it, Steve," I said, after Rick had fastened his seatbelt. "Jump in and take the left middle seat. I'll be right behind you."

Once again, as I pushed the throttle forward, the plane rapidly gained speed, rising up on the steps of the floats like a speedboat skipping along the surface of the water at full speed. With less fuel and a lighter load on board this time, I expected we'd fly at 40 knots.

I held the ailerons in the full-right position to counteract the wind lift on the right, upwind wing. Almost immediately, a violent gust of wind hit us, lifting the right float clear of the water. The gust lasted only a second but was followed by an even stronger one, blasting the right side of the plane and throwing the right wing high in the air. The right and then even the left float lifted clear of the water. We were flying, but at an airspeed insufficient to remain airborne, and with most of the lift coming from the right wing.

Ten feet in the air, the airplane rolled to the left, losing what little lift it had as the gust of wind died, dropping the plane into the river. The left wing struck the water first; the plane cartwheeled onto its back to land upside down in the lake just outside the river's mouth. Fortunately, no one was injured, but the cabin was rapidly filling with ice-cold lake water.

Just before my head went under water I yelled to the others to get out; upside-down, the plane was rapidly settling into the lake. Steve made it out first, climbing out of the submerging cabin and up onto one of the floats. I quickly followed to make way for Rick in the copilot's seat—he couldn't get out until I did.

My first reaction to an ice-cold bath is to gasp, but when you're upside-down being pulled underwater headfirst, the last thing you want to do is gasp. Uncontrollably, I gasped anyway—and surfaced spluttering and choking to cling to the float. Seeing Steve, I climbed up alongside him. Twenty seconds later I felt a pull on my boot as Rick made his escape from the cabin and climbed up to join us.

So there we were, soaking wet in a 35 knot wind, perched like sea gulls on the overturned float 50 feet from shore. The top of the cabin was resting on the bottom of the shoal and wasn't going anywhere, but we had to get to land quickly or we'd freeze.

There was a small settlement of cabins at the mouth of the river that was used as a fish camp by the nearby village of Kakhonak. If anyone had been watching, they might have seen us crash. Searching the settlement for any sign of life, I saw one man standing in an open doorway looking back at me. He waved and disappeared inside the cabin, soon reappearing wearing foul weather clothing and knee-length rubber boots. Another man followed from the cabin to a fishing boat tied up inside the river mouth. After 20 minutes, the boat edged carefully up to the floats and we climbed aboard, one at a time.

Invited into the cabin, we stripped and wrung out our drenched clothing as best we could, gratefully accepting the dry pants, shirts, and jackets offered by the two men who had rescued us, their wives, and children. Since there was no telephone in the camp, one of the men volunteered to drive his three-wheeled ATV to Kakhonak to call the lodge. In the meantime, the wives offered us sandwiches, cookies, and hot coffee. Rick was showing signs of shock and hypothermia: pale skin, loss of concentration, and shivering badly. We made him put on an extra sweater and sit down next to the cabin heater.

Dry, fed, safe, I wandered down to the beach to look at my poor airplane lying upside down in the lake. What had gone wrong? Why hadn't I been able to get the wing back down? Why had it uncontrollably flipped over in mid-air?

The natives drove us to the village, where Reuben was already waiting with the old 180, having landed in the village floatplane pond away from the violent waves on the big lake. The pond was large enough to land and take off directly into the wind and we were all safely back at the lodge in another 20 minutes.

After a sleepless night, I'd figured out the reason for this accident. For the past eight years I'd been flying Cessnas with factory-designed wings in all kinds of weather. This was the first time I'd used the high-lift STOL conversion in a strong crosswind. No wonder the wing flew before it was supposed to—it was now designed that way.

The STOL conversion rerigged the aileron controls on the wings so that they drooped along with the flaps. When the flaps were lowered ten degrees to increase lift on the wing, the ailerons drooped seven degrees, further increasing lift. When the flaps went to twenty degrees, the ailerons followed down to fourteen, increasing the lift even more—and I regularly used twenty degrees for takeoff as recommended by the factory. With the aileron already drooped fourteen degrees, there simply wasn't enough control left in high crosswinds to counteract the extra lift generated by a gust.

Pilots must report all accidents to both the FAA and the National Transportation Safety Board. When I sat down to write this report, under the heading "What do you think caused the accident?" I documented in detail how the Robertson STOL conversion had contributed to the instability of the plane, explaining how I'd received no training from the company on operating in cross wind conditions, nor had the Operators Manual mentioned it.

I have yet to hear from either the FAA or the National Transportation and Safety Board on this. They listed the accident as pilot error and let it go at that.

CHAPTER 27

The last week of August was our busiest of the entire season. Alaska Outdoors had advertised in Japan through a local Japanese travel agent in Hokaido, who booked a group of 16 Japanese for the week, including himself as interpreter. After the new guests had been shown to their rooms and had unpacked, Hayashi, the interpreter, called them back downstairs to the living room, where Mary issued each of them an Alaskan fishing license. Since only Hayashi could understand and speak both languages, he was in constant attendance as each guest was called upon to answer the questions asked on the license application. A few of the younger men in the group understood a little English and tried desperately to communicate, but invariably Hayashi had to help out.

After lunch the guests presented the girls with some simple Japanese children's games and showed us how to use them. One consisted of a small wooden ball tied by a string to a stick with saucer-shaped cups on each end, similar to a small croquet mallet. The object was to bounce the ball from cup to cup by rotating the stick so that first one cup and then the other caught the ball. It required considerable hand-eye coordination, and some of the guests were quite good at it.

Not to be outdone, Angie and Liz brought out one of our own local games they'd picked up in school, and showed the Japanese how to play. As simple as the first, this game also requires coordination between hand and eye. Consisting of two small beanbags connected by a three-foot-long piece of string, the object is to grasp the string in the center and get the two beanbags spinning in opposite directions about your hand. Both Angie and Liz were masters at it and delighted in demonstrating their skill to our new guests.

After lunch I drove them to the Newhalen River to fish. The large salmon run was far from over, but by now these fish had already been in fresh water for six to seven weeks and most of them were already well along in their spawning cycle. When first in from the sea in late June to mid-July, sockeye salmon are firm, silvery, and extremely strong battlers when hooked on a fishing rod. However, their biological change starts with their first taste of fresh water. They stop eating and slowly start to weaken. The bodies turn a bright red while the heads turn green. A white fungus starts to grow in patches on their skin, particularly around their heads, and the flesh turns from a bright red to dull white.

I explained this to the interpreter, emphasizing the fact that these fish were no longer edible and should be released if caught. We were actually going after rainbow trout, arctic char, and grayling, but since a small percent of the salmon might still be fresh, I warned the fishermen to keep only the ones still showing silver or pink sides and to release those with green heads and bright-red bodies. As we topped the last hill in the truck and started down toward the river, the fishermen got their first look at an Alaskan salmon stream in full production.

It was like a hatchery. The river was literally alive with thousands of fish clearly visible in the crystalline water. Every few seconds one of the salmon would pull away from the school and leap frantically through the air, landing on its side with a large splash and reappearing a second or two later to leap again three, four, five times. It's a spectacular sight, particularly for the newcomer; those guys were ecstatic, talking and shouting excitedly as they pointed out each six- to-eight-pound fish dancing across the smooth surface of the river.

There was no use trying to get them to try for the trout or char or grayling, so Reuben and I outfitted them with flies for salmon fishing and let them go at it. Five of the party were fly-fishermen, and went right to work casting into the huge school of fish. Since this particular type of salmon would only strike on flies, the spin fishermen had to fasten lead sinkers to their lines to enable them to cast flies.

The Japanese people apparently consume large amounts of fish, and here, in ten minutes, they'd caught enough for dinner with enough left over for breakfast, too. All the prior discussion on our catch-and-release policy was forgotten in the fishing frenzy. Twelve spawners soon lay dead on the river bank, but their soft flabby flesh, slimy skin, green heads, and bright-red bodies all showed they were well past eating. But the Japanese had never seen fish like this before—and, as for our catch-and-release policy, they'd never released a fish alive before in their entire lives. We ended up bringing 16 fish back to the lodge, half of them females stuffed with skeins of fresh ripe salmon eggs.

After dinner that evening, Mary and I had our first lesson in the caste system of modern Japan and how it serves to get everything done. Among the guests, a few were in their sixties, successful businessmen and obviously in charge. Another half were between 45 and 55, also probably well-established in business but who treated the older guys with courtesy and respect.

The rest of the group were between 30 and 45. These younger men, mostly fly-fishermen, were probably somewhere along the middle-management ladder and acted accordingly. They became the helpers when chores such as fish cleaning were necessary. Hayashi, as interpreter, communicated with all.

That evening Hayashi announced to us that Mr. Ishikawa, one of the older men in the party, was a master chef who owned several restaurants in Japan. He'd brought a large assortment of Japanese foods and would like to prepare a few meals for us. This, Hayashi explained, was why they'd kept the fish that afternoon. Mr. Ishikawa was hoping to practice his culinary skills for all of us.

I could almost hear the bells go off in Mary's head as she pictured someone else taking over her kitchen, but she bravely smiled and said it would be an honor to have someone with so much experience share the cooking. Mr. Ishikawa dispatched

151

his crew of volunteers to strip the salmon eggs one by one from the skeins brought home that afternoon and soon he had a marvellous batch of salmon caviar curing in a brine of his own concoction. The volunteers then cleaned the fish and put them into the refrigerator in a covered pan. Mary refrained from saying anything about the way those old spawners smelled; after all, Mr. Ishikawa was a master chef and should know what he was doing.

Before deciding on where to fish the next day, I had another long talk with Hayashi about our catch-and-release policy. We had a good fresh run of silver salmon in the Mulchatna River so I could promise our guests plenty of fresh fish, but they, in turn, had to promise to release any rainbow, char, or grayling they caught. After explaining to the group, Hayashi assured me that my philosophy was understood and would be honored. And it was.

In the kitchen the next evening, however, the forces of East and West clashed head on. My own job before dinner is to stay out in the living room and swap stories with the guests until Mary announces dinner is ready.

According to Mary, Mr. Ishikawa and three younger volunteers joined her and Connie in the kitchen, where they were preparing a casserole for the rest of the staff who had heard of the Japanese dinner and requested a substitute.

The first thing on Mr. Ishikawa's menu was a delicious hors d'oeuvres of salmon caviar and crackers, accompanied by an excellent Suntory whiskey. Things were going beautifully until the chef opened the refrigerator and took out his salmon. After one sniff of the malodorous pulpy mush in the bottom of the pan, he rushed to the garbage can with the entire mess, wailing as he went.

Hayashi, ever alert for problems, rushed to the kitchen to see what went wrong. After talking to Mr. Ishikawa, Hayashi approached Mary. "The chef says the fish is rotten. He will not cook rotten fish."

Mary nodded; she knew very well they were rotten.

"What can we do? The meal is destroyed. Can you help us, Mama-san?"

Mary thought for a moment. "We have some shrimp in the freezer," she said. "Will that do?"

Hayashi explained Mary's idea to the chef and, by the time she returned with the shrimp, he was all smiles again. Assuming it was her job to prepare the shrimp, Mary poured cooking oil into a large wok and put it on the stove to heat.

The chef already had a large pot of soup heating on another burner and planned to use a third for rice water. Now there were two cooks on one stove, Mary in a colored apron with a kerchief over her hair, and Mr. Ishikawa in a full white apron and chef's hat, each talking to their respective assistants as the meal preparation continued. Hayashi failed to recognize the explosive potential and returned to the living room.

Filling the rice pot with water, the Japanese chef placed it on the stove and lit the gas under it. As the rice water and shrimp oil warmed up on adjacent burners, so did the chef, protesting in Japanese that the rice water would boil over into the oil. Mary, not understanding a word, turned away to help Connie with a salad for the crew. Hayashi, now tuned to Mr. Ishikawa's voice, ran back into the kitchen.

"Mama-san," he explained to Mary, "the chef says his rice water will boil over into your hot oil."

"Not if he turns down the flame," Mary said.

"It will boil over anyway, Mama-san."

"I've boiled water for rice hundreds of times, and it never boiled over."

After explaining this to the chef, Hayashi turned to Mary. "He says it will boil over, Mama-san. It will splatter in the oil."

"WELL, ALL RIGHT!" Mary said, throwing her potholder on the unused griddle. "YOU DO IT!" and stalked out of the kitchen.

Out in the front room, meanwhile, the rest of us sat transfixed over the argument coming from the kitchen, smiling at each other since there wasn't any other way to communicate without Hayashi.

After walking around to cool off, Mary returned to the kitchen, where, sure enough, the rice water was boiling merrily away, splashing over the side of the pot onto the burner from which the wok of hot oil had just been removed. Mr. Ishikawa smiled contentedly, but bustled his assistants out of the way to make room for Mary at the counter. The rest of the meal preparation went without incident.

Dinner was remarkably pleasant. The Japanese soup, made of a fish base with vegetables and noodles, was absolutely superb. Mary's shrimp with Mr. Ishikawa's rice and vegetables was excellent, and for dessert, good old American apple pie. After dinner, Mary even invited Mr. Ishikawa to help prepare other meals during their stay.

The episode of the spoiled salmon seemed to have made a significant impression. After that, I had no more trouble with my catch-and-release policy, which, admittedly, has always been more conservative than required by the fish and game regulations.

That evening, as I was assigning the fishing areas for our guests on the following day, one of the older men interrupted me. I had planned to send a group to a new location and had just described the area and the fishing, but warned them it was to be a strictly catch-and-release outing.

"Excuse me, Mr. Ted," the older man questioned. "Must we release all fish in this new river?"

"Yes," I said.

"Please excuse me again, but is this Alaska law or Ted's law?"

"Ted's law," I said.

CHAPTER 28

Keith and Marge Russell of Ohio, guests at the lodge in early September, were asleep in their room at the northeast corner of the lodge when Marge, a light sleeper, woke at about three o'clock in the morning to the crackle of fire. The room was filled with an eerie red light; the reflections of flames leaped along the wall opposite the window, rising from floor to ceiling in fiery curtains of light and shadow. Shaking Keith awake, Marge grabbed their bathrobes while her husband rushed across the hall to bang on our door.

Pulling on a pair of trousers, I raced outside, grabbing the always handy extinguisher, but the fire was already raging out of control. It was the generator shack again; unbelieving, I stared at an inferno that had already engulfed the building in flames. All four walls burned fiercely, and I stood transfixed as the roof collapsed into the center of the structure. The night was cool and clear, with a strong northerly wind blowing from the fire directly toward the lodge—just as it had been at the previous fire. Once again we were in danger of losing everything.

Shaking off my feeling of helpless incredulity, I ran to fetch the garden hose and started spraying the corner of the lodge closest to the fire—just as I'd done before. As soon as the first guest arrived, I shoved the nozzle at him and ran around to the fuel tanks to shut off the supply line feeding raw diesel oil into the fire—again, just as I'd done before.

155

Mary stopped long enough in the lodge to alert all the rest of the guests and call for the FAA fire truck. Together we ran to the dog kennel and opened the door, allowing all three beagles to escape. They had been huddled together next to the door, as far from the searing heat as possible.

Performance of the FAA fire truck crew was considerably improved this time. No cobwebs or dirt flew up when we stripped the hoses off the truck, and within seconds, operator Jim Coffee had water surging through the new hoses toward the fire. Taking hold of the first hose, I fought against the force of the water as it shot out of the nozzle, directing the blast first at the lodge, then at the fuel tanks, finally at the fire itself. By this time the shack had burned to the ground, but the charred roof and wall supports continued to blaze until sufficient water had been used to cool down the entire site.

I located another generator in Seattle and had power restored in 36 hours. The new unit was again sitting out in the yard and exposed to the elements, but rather than take time to rebuild another shack that late in the season, we bought a small metal building from Sears for shelter until next spring.

Three days later, the same Alaskan State Trooper arrived to inspect the ashes of the fire, with as little success as before. If he suspected arson, there was no proof left. The only difference between this fire and the one we'd had only 15 months before was the condition of the generator; this time it had been running, last time it had been turned off.

The day after the fire, after preparing breakfast for everyone on our gas-fired kitchen range, Mary went back to our bedroom, lay down on the bed, pulled the blankets over her head—and stayed there until my Uncle Bill arrived on the afternoon flight. The long days of work without a break, coupled with all our unexpected hardships, had finally caught up with her.

"Where's Mary?" Bill asked as he climbed the stairs and entered the front room. Bill and Mary had liked each other the first time they'd met, the friendship developing more with each of his visits to Iliamna. He sensed there was something wrong when she didn't meet him at the door.

"In the bedroom," I said. "Why don't you go back and say hello while I take these new guests upstairs?" Half an hour later Mary and Bill reappeared in the front room, Mary looking refreshed and smiling again. Uncle Bill has always been a confidence builder.

Bill is my mother's brother. An outdoorsman all his life, he's the man who took me out to a local pond at the age of five and started me off catching sunfish and perch with worms and a cane pole. As I grew up, he introduced me to fly-fishing for trout, shotgunning for ruffed grouse, and finally hunting white-tailed deer in the Green Mountains of Vermont. A lean six-footer in his youth, he has been an active sportsman all his life. Due to turn 65 that fall, the gleam in his eye for the outdoor life still shone brightly.

Uncle Bill first started coming to Alaska in 1972, the first year I moved to Kodiak Island. I had settled my family into the government quarters provided at the Coast Guard Base on the island and almost immediately started exploring the hunting and fishing possibilities. When Bill and his wife Cynthia arrived late in the summer, he and I fished for silver salmon and hunted deer and elk together. In 1973, on his second trip north, this time alone, our exploring brought us to Iliamna for the first time, where we tasted the thrills of rainbow trout fishing and caribou hunting.

On Bill's third trip, Cynthia also stayed at home. We were sitting around the dinner table on the day he arrived when Uncle Bill confessed he didn't know why he'd had to come again. "I've been here twice in two years now," he said. "Of course it's always nice to see you, Ted, but Alaska's a long way from Vermont. I don't know what called me back."

Two days later we were fishing for silver salmon in Saltery Lake on Kodiak just a mile upstream from the salt water of Ugak Bay. Fresh silvers milled about in schools along the lakeshore, performing their ritual of selecting mates and spawning beds, and as I taxied the airplane toward the beach we could see hundreds of fish swimming around in the clear lake water.

Bill and I each chose a spot along the beach and began casting streamer patterns into the midst of the 10- to-12-pound fish. From a hundred yards away, I suddenly heard Bill cry out, "Now

I know!"

Looking over, I saw Uncle Bill thigh-deep in the water, his flyrod now arched in a 90-degree bow against the Kodiak sky. A fat 10-pound salmon leaped clear of the lake surface a hundred feet off shore once, twice, a third time, stripping line from Bill's reel and making its clicker scream in the still evening air.

"Now I know," he cried again. "Now I know why I had to come back!"

Uncle Bill, as he's affectionately called by all our guests, hasn't missed a year without visiting me in Alaska. Since his retirement as General Manager of Central Vermont Power Company, his visits have brought us a lifelong treasury of fly-fishing knowledge and experience. As for Aunt Cynthia, she brings us an inexhaustible fund of good sense and good humor when she accompanies Bill north.

"You know, Ted," Uncle Bill told me one day a few years back. "I've finally figured it all out. I'll be a year older next summer whether I come north and fish with you or stay home—so I'll come fishing as long as I can."

CHAPTER 29

Angus Cameron—sportsman, author, publisher, and master fish and game chef—was approaching 70 years of age that fall. A stockily built man of average height, he looked every bit the part as he stepped off the airplane onto the gravel ramp at the Iliamna airport. Wearing wool trousers, checkered shirt and bolo tie, stylish woolen jacket, and a soft-brimmed fishing hat, he would have made an imposing figure in any gathering of fishermen. His wife Sheila—several inches shorter and five-stone lighter, with sparkling eyes, light step, and nattily dressed in a tartaned suit—fairly skipped alongside her husband. Recognizing the Iliaska Lodge sign on the side door of the truck, they headed directly toward Mary and me, hands outstretched in greeting.

Angus and I had exchanged several letters during the past year since being introduced through the mail by Eric Leiser, owner of The River Gate, a fly-fishing shop in New York State. Hearing of our attempt to establish a fly-fishing-only lodge in Alaska, Eric had felt that Angus, his friend and publisher, might be of assistance with advertising. We met for the first time on that mild fall afternoon and have become fast friends ever since.

Although they'd never visited the Iliamna or Bristol Bay area before, Angus and Sheila were not strangers to Alaska, having spent several months camped in the foothills of the Brooks Range with big game guide Bud Helmericks in the 1950s. With two young children at the time, they'd lived on a primitive level,

159

subsisting on the fish and game available in the area. Both were now anxious to see as much of our part of the state as possible, in particular the trophy fishing in September.

We wasted no time getting started. The next seven days, we fished our way from one trophy spot to another. Mary joined us on the stream when she could, and the rainbow trout fishing couldn't have been better. Both Angus and Sheila caught several fish over 10 pounds—plus dozens of fish in the three- to five-pound class—hooking them, landing them, and then cheerfully releasing them.

"Don't those rainbows put up a good fight," Angus said later. "Pound for pound, they're as good on a flyrod as any Atlantic salmon I've ever seen."

I've never fished for Atlantic salmon, so I can't compare them to our rainbows, but here was a man who'd taken many salmon from rivers on both sides of the Atlantic and who could judge the fish fairly, saying that the Iliamna rainbow trout were equal in strength and fighting ability to that fabled of all freshwater sport fish, the Atlantic salmon.

"It's everything you said it was," Angus said one evening after dinner. "I know a lot of Atlantic salmon fishermen on the East Coast who'd certainly like to try this."

"Wouldn't Ed Ruestow of West Hartford love it here, Angus?" Sheila said. "He's one of the most ardent salmon fishermen we know." Ed has since landed rainbows up to 12 pounds at Iliaska Lodge.

"And that pair from the Tunxis Club, Mack Wallace and Lew Stone," Angus said. "We'll have to tell them about this place too." Mack has since landed several trout over 10 pounds, including one taken and photographed by the fabled Lee Wulff, who happened to be fishing Lower Talarik Creek on the same day Mack was there. But as hard as Mack tries, he still hasn't beaten Lew, who landed a 14-pound rainbow trout on his first day's fishing in Iliamna.

Later that week, Angus, Sheila, and I were fishing one of the local streams for the rainbow trout we could see darting back and forth among the hundreds of spawning sockeye salmon in the water. But where there are salmon, there too will be bear.

Part way into the afternoon, as Sheila and I were fishing along the same stretch, with Angus downstream about a hundred feet, a particularly fine specimen of *Ursus horribilis* stepped out of the forested riverbank a few hundred yards downstream of Angus. Walking into the water, the bear waded across to the gravel bar on the other end of which Sheila and I were standing. Telling Sheila to stay where she was, I started walking down stream with the current.

"Better reel in, Angus," I called. "He looks pretty big, and I don't think we can bluff this one."

Angus, so intent on the trout he hadn't noticed the bear, glanced downstream to his left. We'd seen a few four- to five-hundred pound bears on the river already, but none to compare with this behemoth. Angus quickly moved out of the river and started backing upstream toward me. He couldn't take his eyes off that bear.

"Hello, Mr. Bear," I called, to let the bear know we knew he was there. "Nice to see you on the river this afternoon."

It was a fine coastal grizzly. Light brown to tan, it had the typical silver-tipped hair of the species and a pronounced hump over the front shoulders. This one also had a huge pot belly from a gluttonous appetite. It had obviously been feeding on salmon for the last three months and now carried a sufficient layer of fat to see him through his winter hibernation. I guessed his weight at a thousand pounds.

"Don't worry, Angus," I called. "The bear is more afraid of you than you are of it."

"The hell it is," Angus said, and continued moving upstream.

"Fishing has been fine today," I told the bear. "We've caught some nice trout, but of course we wouldn't take any of your salmon. If you keep moving toward us like that, we'll even let you fish here. But the fishing is just as good downstream. Go on down there and try. Please?"

The bear walked across the gravel to the water's edge and started slowly upstream toward us. "I think, Angus, I'd start walking upstream to Sheila now," I said, and we both started backing away from the approaching bear. Angus didn't wait for a second invitation.

"Hello, Mr. Bear," I called again. "We were just leaving. You're welcome to take our place and fish here if you insist," and, ceding the gravel bar to the bear, all three of us waded across the stream to the opposite shore.

"You know, Ted," Angus said later that evening. "I have a confession to make. As you were talking to the bear, I started backing upstream toward Sheila as you advised. But the embarrassing thing is, I didn't stop backing until I noticed Sheila was between me and the bear."

CHAPTER 30

In late September I realized we still hadn't been paid by Alaska Outdoors for the 16 Japanese we'd entertained in August. They owed us over $12,000 for the Japanese party alone, and the bill was now a month overdue. We were desperately short of money again that year, having had to replace both an airplane and generator. But when I called and asked for Jim Repine, I was told that he didn't work there anymore. Jim had been one of the original partners in the business—what could have happened to make him quit?

"Let me speak with Evan Swensen then," I said. Evan was president of Alaska Outdoors. After a slight delay, Evan came on the line and I asked him when we could expect payment on the invoice we'd sent for the Japanese group.

"The check should be in the mail in a day or two, Ted."

"We're really hurting down here for cash, Evan," I explained. "We submitted that invoice over a month ago—and what about the three we sent after that one? When will we get paid for them?"

"No problem," Evan assured me. "Don't worry—we're good for it."

Something was wrong—I could feel it. I tried calling Jim at home, but no one answered. Next I tried to call Bill Holden, who'd also left Alaska Outdoors, but I couldn't reach him either.

Mary and I had really started to worry when, a week later, Jim called back. "Hello, Ted. Heard you were trying to get hold

163

of me."

"You can be a hard man to find sometimes, Jim," I said, and got right to the point. "What happened between you and Alaska Outdoors?"

"Evan and I had a falling out," Jim said cautiously.

"Tell me one thing—are they short of money?"

"Very short. If the loan they've applied for from the State of Alaska doesn't come through, they'll be in really tough shape. How much do they owe you?"

"About $15,000."

"If I were you, I'd go after them tooth and nail for it. Sue them if you have to—and soon. It looks like they may go under."

Great news. Here was the man who'd encouraged us to sign on with Alaska Outdoors now advising me to sue his own company for payment.

It didn't take Mary and me long to decide what to do. I took off for Anchorage at once and went straight to Evan Swensen's office. Turning up on his doorstep apparently did the trick; after a lot of hemming and hawing, Evan reluctantly signed a check for slightly over $12,000, the exact balance due on the Japanese party. When I asked him about our other invoices, he admitted he needed a little extra time to find the money.

I drove straight to the bank to deposit the funds in our account. Fortunately, the check didn't bounce. Eventually we received some of the rest of the money—but in the form of credits, not cash. We later found out that Alaska Outdoors had paid very few of its debts that summer. A year later they declared bankruptcy, still owing a lot of money to a lot of people.

Thus ended our association with Alaska Outdoors. Although we didn't get all the money owed us, on balance we made out pretty well. Several of the guests they'd introduced to the lodge have returned on their own, some more than once, and the experience I'd gained observing how television shows are produced and how sportsmen's shows are run would prove valuable in the future.

Another important thing we learned: never sign another contract giving a 20% commission for booking services. We couldn't pay that much and hope to become profitable.

One of the guests first sent to the lodge by Alaska Outdoors was Harm Saville of Rowley, Massachusetts. Harm liked Iliaska so much that he returned seven years in a row, the last five with his buddy Keith Laver of Ontario. Harm and Keith tried each month of our season and finally settled on the fall rainbow fishing as their favorite time. Mary and I cherish the friends like Harm and Keith that we've made at Iliaska.

Randall Kaufmann returned in October to sample our fall rainbow fishing, bringing four paying guests with him: Joe Demeter of Pasadena, John Hickox of Portland, and Bill Bohannon and Ginny Hagstrom of June Lake, California. Although the four men in the group were all experienced fly-fishermen, Ginny was a beginner. Bill Bohannon had taught her how to cast a flyrod the week before in their backyard; we started her fishing for grayling in the Newhalen the afternoon of their arrival. She landed six fish and was off to a good start.

After the first day, the fall weather turned miserable. Strong winds and rainstorms lashed Lake Iliamna, and we spent part of two days inside the lodge watching the wind gauge bounce between 40 and 50 knots. As soon as the weather cleared, I flew Randall and his group to Lower Talarik Creek for some rainbow trout fishing, where each of them hooked and landed several fish between 8 and 10 pounds.

Ginny had the hardest time of it. Although the wind had dropped enough to allow flying, it was still blowing 20 knots at the creek, and she was having a difficult time casting more than 15 feet. Moving her upstream to a spot protected by a bluff, where the wind wasn't howling quite so badly, I encouraged her to try again and, before the day ended, she'd finally hooked and landed her first rainbow trout on a flyrod—it weighed eight pounds.

Randall took the largest fish of the guests, a 14-pound male in spawning colors that photographed beautifully. I spent the day walking back and forth among the five guests, who were all fishing along a half-mile stretch of river. As I moved from client to client, I would drop my own fly in the water, fishing along as I walked downstream. Using a black Iliaska muddler pattern (the same fly that Mary had used to land her big one last year),

I struck a particularly large fish and played it to a section of beach hundreds of yards from any of the other fishermen. The male trout measured 34 inches and weighed 16 pounds, the largest rainbow I'd ever taken. I slipped it back into the water unnoticed, put away my flyrod, lit a small fire under the bluff, and made a pot of coffee. Eventually, as each guest smelled the smoke, they came over and joined me out of the wind.

I didn't say anything about the big fish for several days. One night, after the guests had all left for the year, Mary and I were having dinner together.

"Angus suggested we start a fishing log, Mary," I said. "A ledger of some type to keep track of the larger fish we catch. What do you think?"

"Good idea," she said. "I remember he said that most of the Atlantic salmon camps have them."

"I agree with Angus," I said, thinking of my 16-pounder. "There should be a record kept of the significant fish taken each week at the lodge. We'll get a stout ledger book and ask each guest to write in it when they make a good catch. We'll include the date, name of the stream, species, length and estimated weight, the fly used, and the fisherman's name and home town."

It is called The Book now, and the entries are referred to as Book Fish at the lodge. The first entry reads as follows: 11 October, 1979 on Lower Talarik Creek. Rainbow trout 34", 16 pounds. Released. #4 black muddler, weighted. Ted Gerken, Iliamna, Alaska.

Chapter 31

W ith the long hours, constant worry, and one disaster after another, Mary's nerves were getting jumpy. One evening, after a particularly exhausting day—not only for Mary and me but even for the guests—we'd all retired early. Sunset in mid-September comes about eight o'clock in the evening, with twilight lingering on for another hour or so. By 9:30 the lodge was quiet, the generator secured, and everyone in bed. Even the beagles dozed quietly in their kennel.

Only the skies were still busy. Nick Sias was a commercial pilot for Alaska Bush Carrier, an air taxi operator based in Anchorage. A tall, spare man in his forties, he had an ardent enthusiasm for Mary's cooking and would always drop in when passing through Iliamna.

Nick was flying a Cessna 206 on wheels that evening. When the approach of darkness caught him in the vicinity of Iliamna, he decided not to wake us up by landing out at the State Airport and calling the lodge for a ride, but, instead, to land on the straight stretch of road in front of the post office only a quarter mile away and taxi to the lodge. Nick knew that I occasionally used the road as an airstrip during the winter.

After he'd landed on the road, Nick used the powerful, sealed-beam landing lights on his plane to guide his way to the lodge. The road ends in a wide gravel yard between the lodge, shop, generator shack, and hangar: a cul-de-sac large enough to maneuver airplanes and vehicles around. When Nick reached the cul-de-sac, he turned his aircraft around to face back up the road by locking the left brake and gunning the 300 horsepower engine. His plane spun around with a deafening roar; the bright beam of his lights raked our bedroom window; Mary leapt out of bed screaming, "Fire! Fire! The generator shack's on fire!"

"It can't be the generator shack. It burned down two weeks ago!" I shouted, jumping up to race to the window. "It must be the hangar!"

Just then Nick pulled the throttle back, killed the engine, and turned off his lights. Darkness and silence filled the room so abruptly I heard Mary gasp with surprise. "It's all right, Mary," I said as soon as my eyes had adjusted to the moonlit yard. "Some SOB just drove up in his airplane."

Mary was furious. "If they want lodging tonight, they can sleep in the dog kennel," she said, and dropped back into bed.

Three minutes later I heard footsteps on the outside stairs. Now fully awake and dressed again, I walked out to the front room to confront our new arrival. Several other guests, including Jim Zamlich, Steve Hill, Rick Arena, and Stan Engel from the San Francisco Bay area, and Jerry Melcher from Anchorage all came downstairs to see what had happened, arriving just as Nick opened the door.

"Am I too late for dinner?" he asked.

Most of us were barefoot. The few who'd taken time to dress had shirts hanging out of their trousers. The rest of us wore bathrobes, and we all had rumpled hair. As Nick gazed at the circle of faces staring at him, he realized what he'd done.

"This is Nick Sias, a pilot from Anchorage," I said to the silent ring of guests. "I'd suggest you introduce yourselves tomorrow morning at breakfast and go back to bed now."

Turning to Nick, I said, "Yes, Nick, you're too late for dinner— and you'd better apologize to Mary in the morning or you won't get any breakfast either. You can take a bed in the north room upstairs."

"It's your fault, Mary," I said as I climbed back into bed. "That was Nick in the plane. If you didn't feed him so well, he wouldn't have landed here after dark."

A few days later, Mary shook me awake at dawn. "Wake up, Ted," she was muttering. "Wake up."

"I'm awake." It was partly true.

"There's something wrong with my jaw."

"Sounds okay to me," I said. Sympathy isn't my strong point at 5:00 in the morning.

"It's my jaw—I can't open my mouth."

That woke me up. It was true—she couldn't. Her jaws were clenched so tightly her mouth wouldn't open at all.

"How am I going to brush my teeth?" she mumbled, tears standing in her eyes as she strained to wrench apart her jaws. "How am I going to eat?"

"With a straw?" I suggested.

Mary threw a pillow at me and stormed out to fix breakfast. Whether she could eat or not, there were still seven guests to feed.

One of those guests was Rick Garner, an orthopedic surgeon from Anchorage. After watching Mary sitting at the table trying to poke small bits of scrambled egg through the half-inch gap between her top and bottom teeth created by an overbite, he finally couldn't stand it anymore. "Is there something wrong with your mouth, Mary?" he asked.

"I think my lower jaw must be dislocated," she mumbled. "I can't open it."

"Let me work on it," the doctor volunteered. "I'm not a dentist, but if it's out of joint, I should be able to pop it back in."

Mary accepted Rick's offer gratefully. Eating had become a real problem; while everyone else had finished their plates, Mary was only half done. She pushed her dishes away and motioned to Rick to do what he could.

Rick approached her chair from behind and placed both hands on Mary's jaw, massaging the muscles back and forth from neck to cheekbones. "Your muscles feel tense, Mary," he said. "Try to relax a little so I can get my thumbs between your teeth."

"I'm about as relaxed as I can get, doctor," she muttered.

Rick was a strong man, six feet tall and used to manipulating joints. Taking a firm hold with both hands, he forced Mary's jaw open just enough to get his thumbs into the joint behind her teeth and then tried to move her lower jaw backwards and forwards. Mary cried out in pain, tears swelling from both eyes as Rick relentlessly pushed and pulled at the jaw. After a few minutes of this self-imposed torture, Mary grabbed the doctor's hands and tore them away from her red, tearstained face. Her jaw throbbed with pain. "I'm sorry, doctor," she mumbled, "I can't stand it. Let's give it a rest until this afternoon."

Rick worked on Mary's jaw another five minutes that evening before dinner, but with no more success than in the morning; while we ate steak for supper, Mary had finely ground meat loaf and mashed potatoes. She even had to mash her green peas to eat them—the half-inch gap between her teeth had closed to less than three-eighths of an inch.

The doctor left the next day but Mary's problem was far from over. Convinced that it was nothing more than a dislocation, she next consulted the U.S. Public Health Service doctor who was visiting Iliamna for the Bureau of Indian Affairs. After ten minutes of torture in his chair, Mary again pulled the hands away from her throbbing jaws, unable to stand the pain any longer.

As luck would have it, that week our regular dentist from Anchorage, Ken Wynne, arrived to do some bear hunting on the Peninsula. Ken took one look and knew at once what was wrong. "It's not dislocated, Mary," he said cheerfully. "You have TMJ."

"TMJ?" I asked.

"Traumatic Mandibular Joint. It's stress-related. I'll bet you've been grinding your teeth in your sleep."

"That's ridiculous," Mary almost shouted. "Who ever heard of stress causing something like this?"

"I'm serious," Ken said. "It's one of the effects of prolonged stress. We see it so often these days we even have a name for it now."

"But what can we do?" I wanted to know. This was getting serious—to get rid of stress, we'd have to give up the lodge. Either that or Mary would have to eat through a straw the rest of her life!

"Don't worry," the dentist reassured us. "Literally—the condition will clear up by itself. Next time you're in town, come by my office and I'll fit you with a night-guard to stop the grinding.

Besides, winter's coming and it's your slow season. That will help more than anything else."

Ken was right, of course. The problem did slowly correct itself. One month after Ken's visit, Mary could open her jaws far enough to eat normally again, but it was close to a year before she could get her teeth around a moose steak again.

CHAPTER 32

Mary, what do you want to do for your birthday this year?" I asked. It was early October; the last hunters and fishermen had just left and we were back to only walk-in, overnight guests, but Mary needed a break.

"I'd like to take the girls down to the caribou cabin. I've never seen it, you know," Mary said.

Some people might say that once a woman reaches 33 she should know enough to avoid places like a wilderness hunting cabin. Few women I know would volunteer to pack supplies half a mile from the lake, stay in a dark, unheated camp, sleep on an old army cot donated by a disgruntled BLM firefighter, cook over a camp stove that needed pumping every 15 minutes to maintain a flame, and—worse yet—she and the girls would have to perch on the icy throne of the temporary outhouse we'd hastily built that year. We hadn't had enough time or lumber to build the walls and roof, just dug a hole in the ground and built a box over it with an oval hole cut in its top. At least I'd filed off most of the splinters.

But if that's what she wanted, that's what she'd get. "We can leave next Friday if you like," I said.

The weather was mild for October: temperatures in the thirties and forties, light winds, and little rain or snow. We were reasonably sure the lake at the camp wouldn't freeze over for another week. With the aircraft still on floats, I certainly didn't want to get caught out there with ice starting to form on my runway. As usual, Mary did the packing while I tended to the airplane, and we were airborne by 11:00 on the morning of October 7th, the day before her birthday.

We spotted two small bands of caribou near the cabin that evening, plus a larger group of 40 or more two miles away on the open plain to the southwest. Hunting conditions were ideal, with good visibility and light winds. When a single, medium-sized bull roamed within a quarter mile of camp, I dropped him with a single shot to the neck.

"Can we watch you cut it up?" Angela asked.

"Sure, Angie," I said. "You can help carry some of the meat back to the airplane, too. Right, Mary?"

"They both have backpacks," Mary answered. "I carried plenty of my father's moose meat when I was a girl."

Both daughters watched closely as I field-dressed and quartered the animal. I took time to explain each step, getting them to assist by holding, pulling, and fetching until the job was done. Then I divided up the meat according to size: the lightest load for 8-year-old Elizabeth and gradually heavier loads for Angie and Mary. I took half the animal in my own pack and we started back toward the plane. The girls led the way, holding hands and gabbing like magpies.

The next morning we climbed the knoll behind camp to look around again. The tender and delicious meat of a second caribou was on my mind as I adjusted the focus on my binoculars and started a sweep of the horizon. I saw a few small groups too far away to bother with, but the large group of over 40 was still in the same spot as the night before. They were all lying down, but I knew that hunger would soon start them wandering again.

There was one particular animal in that band that fascinated me—a huge bull with dark heavy antlers and a pure white mane. He was the first to stand and dwarfed the others as, one by one, they all rose to follow the monarch.

What a magnificent animal it was. Constantly moving in and around the herd of cows, calves, and immature bulls, he appeared to monitor their every move, keeping the herd together. When one of the five or six smaller bulls on the periphery approached too closely, the boss would lower his massive rack of horns and run the intruder off a good quarter mile, prodding and jabbing him in the side and rump.

"Mary, come take a look," I said, handing her the binoculars. "It's the biggest bull I've seen out here in seven years."

Mary took the glasses and watched for a minute. "Wow, what a large rack of antlers," she said. "But he's in the rut, Ted. Look how he's acting."

"I know, but look at those horns!" There are times when greed takes precedence over common sense. "I'm going to try to get close enough for a shot. Should be 200 pounds of meat on him."

The animals milled about for half an hour, aimlessly wandering in the area where they'd bedded down for the night. Finally they started feeding slowly into the wind, moving from left to right across the wide valley. A caribou can walk and feed across the tundra at a pace faster than a man can trot, if it wants to. That morning they appeared in no particular hurry, allowing time for me to approach.

The stalk took two hours, and I lost sight of the herd shortly after I descended from the knoll. A converging course brought me almost within range in a section of flat tundra interspersed with low brushy alders. I dropped my pack to make the going easier and started crawling, trying to keep a small group of bushes between myself and where I thought the herd should be. The caribou were spread out and feeding on lichen; the closer I got, the greater the chances that one of them would spot me. In a herd like this one, the cows are more alert to danger than the bulls.

I crawled for 15 minutes, finally making it to a spot directly behind a scrub bush only three feet tall and about two hundred yards away from three cows and a calf. These were the first animals I'd seen since leaving the knoll, and all but one had its head down, feeding around a large opening free from brush and trees. One of the cows was staring straight at my bush.

I lay motionless while the cow watched, the stare-down lasting half a minute or more. Then she trotted out into the middle of the large opening straight toward me. The other three animals in the clearing stopped feeding to follow her, in turn followed by the rest of the herd who'd been hidden by the ring of brush and low trees. Dozens of caribou poured into the clearing, following the lead cow who passed 150 yards in front of me, now running from right to left.

The monstrous herd bull was again in the middle of the pack, standing head and shoulders over the cows. I waited until a clear firing lane opened up and then placed a bullet just behind and below his left front shoulder. The lung shot proved fatal, although he continued to run with the herd a few hundred yards before collapsing.

The crawling I'd done while stalking the bull came back to haunt me in my hour of triumph. As I started to rise from the prone firing position, my right knee twisted painfully inside my water-soaked woolen trousers. I fell back on the tundra with an audible groan.

What a terrible time for a trick knee to act up, I thought, as I rolled over and looked at my leg. It was flexed at a 45-degree angle, and when I pushed downward on the knee with my hands to try to straighten it out, another jolt of pain shot up my thigh.

I'd gone through this before and knew that I couldn't rush things, so I lay back and rested. After 30 minutes on the soggy tundra, I managed to get back up on my feet, pick up the rifle, fetch the pack, and start to limp out across the clearing toward the dead bull.

When first seen from two miles away, it had obviously been the largest animal in the herd; from 150 yards it had dwarfed the smaller cows and calves running along beside it; but now, from only 10 feet away, it was even bigger than I'd imagined. Huge walnut-colored horns sported numerous lighter-tipped points along both branches. Fully 450 pounds or more on the hoof, the whiteness of mane and rump accented the browns and tans on the rest of the hide.

I can skin and quarter an average caribou in half an hour, but this was not a normal animal, and neither was I in the best of shape. An hour later, with the job only half done, I heard a call from the cabin direction. Mary had seen me from the cabin and, with both girls in tow, was on her way to help.

Mary quickly noticed two things as she covered the last 50 feet. First was my limp. That she could sympathize with—but the unmistakably gamy odor coming from the dead animal didn't please her at all. As a chef she was more concerned with the flavor of the meat than the size of the animal. "Hope you like lots of sausage," was all she said.

But my enthusiasm was undampened. This was the finest trophy I'd ever taken; it had the possibility of making the record book. We saved the horns, meat, and hide, packing everything over to the shore of another lake that was only a quarter of a mile away.

Mary's prediction about the meat was true, of course, and I was to hear about that strong flavor for months afterward. She tried every way she could think of to hide the gaminess, but most of it ended up in sausage. Not a scrap was wasted, but she made me promise not to shoot another bull in the rut again, regardless of size.

The horns measured 387 points, just 13 shy of the record book, due primarily to an imbalance between the two main beams. If we hadn't had to subtract the difference in measurements between the two sides from the total, it would have measured well over 400 and made the book. They're now nailed to the hangar wall at the lodge.

"And think of what I did for all those younger bulls, Mary," I said after we returned to the cabin. "They're old enough to mate, but none of them was big enough to command any attention from the cows in that herd. Now the herd will split up into smaller groups and the younger males will each get one."

Even in the face of such a reasonable argument, Mary remained adamant. "And you shot him on my birthday, too!"

CHAPTER 33

T
here is a smallish creek that originates in the low hills to the northwest of Lake Iliamna and glides smoothly through shallow tundra valleys toward the big lake. During September and October some of the largest native rainbow trout in the world leave Lake Iliamna to swim up the shallow, gravel-bedded meanders of this lovely stream. Big fish and small waters—an anomaly of nature that freshwater fishermen are unable to resist—have turned Lower Talarik Creek into a fisherman's paradise.

Uncle Bill and I first discovered this creek back in 1973 when we were flying over the area looking for likely places to fish. The first day—with ten-pound rainbows darting around our feet, leaping, swirling, driving us frantic with the desire to hook one of them—I got skunked. I couldn't believe it. I tried every fly in my vest, every technique learned in 30 years of fly-fishing, and still nothing. Bill managed to take one nice fish on a bright streamer but that was all.

There were four fishermen from Enchanted Lake Lodge on the stream that day, guided by Ed Siler, a six-foot, angular man already in his 60's. Thoroughly discouraged, I sat on the bank for awhile that afternoon and watched Ed fish. After he'd hooked, played, and released a 12-pounder, I walked over to him and asked what fly he was using.

"It's a dark pattern," he said, showing me a blackish, stream-

179

worn handful of hair and feathers, "and working pretty well today. I fish it near the bottom."

Unfortunately, we had nothing like it. All our flies were bright and colorful streamers designed to imitate salmon fry and smolt. But we were learning.

I didn't return to the creek until the fall of 1977, our first year with the lodge. I came well supplied with dark flies this time, all tied to imitate the natural sculpin found in the Iliamna watershed. Black, brown, and olive, alone or in combination, proved to be the best colors, but something bothered me. There weren't that many sculpin in the creek to attract so many big fish, and they weren't acting as if they were exceptionally hungry, so why did these fish leave the lake each September to swim up this minor tundra stream? Why leave the relative safety of deep water to seek this shallow tributary? Why leave the abundant food supply of pygmy whitefish in Lake Iliamna for the relative barrenness of the creek?

If this were April, I could understand it, since rainbow trout spawn in the spring. But would they come upriver in September to spawn in April? Or were some of them spawning in the winter?

Twice we've caught females that were hooked too deeply to release and brought them back to the lodge for breakfast. On cleaning them, we'd found large skeins of almost fully developed eggs inside the abdominal cavity. Could these fish carry such well-developed eggs from September all the way through the winter, waiting to spawn in April? And even if they could, why would they?

In January of 1977, during an extremely mild winter, when neither Lake Iliamna nor many of its tributaries froze over, two of the local natives living in Newhalen netted over a hundred large rainbow trout in Lower Talarik Creek. They were spotted doing it, fortunately, and reported to the wildlife protection officers.

An overflow in March of 1984 proved that these large rainbow trout live in the stream all winter despite ice build-ups. The creek was frozen over, with only a minimal flow of water between the surface ice and the bottom of the stream. An unusually warm winter storm brought wind and rain into the area, flooding Lower Talarik Creek. There wasn't enough space below the ice to hold all the extra water, and it surged over the top of the ice. About 70 large rainbows got caught in the overflow and perished on top of the ice when the flooding subsided.

There's relatively little food within the stream during the winter, and the near-freezing water temperatures are too low to induce much activity anyway. Apparently the eggs develop when these fish are feeding heavily in Lake Iliamna, before entering their spawning streams in September. Whatever the reason for the September migration, we fishermen reap the benefit, for these are the wildest fighting fish I've ever tangled with.

I've fished Lower Talarik Creek with some of the best fly fishermen I've known, those for whom I reserve the title Master Fly-Fisherman. The one thing that separates these sportsmen from all others is concentration. These Master Fishermen seldom take their eyes off the river, always studying its surface for signs of life below. Oblivious to everything but fish, they are true predators, as alert to opportunity as any other animal that depends on its wits to survive.

One of these is a carpenter from the San Francisco Bay area named Gary Cano. About 5'6" tall, with a wiry frame and dark complexion, Gary looks like an average American. But among fly-fisherman, he's anything but average. In the fall of 1978, Gary spent a week at Iliaska with two friends, Jim Zamlich and Bart Fisk. Although I was doing most of the guiding that year, I was not with the party on their first trip to the creek.

"How did it go, fellas?" I asked that night at Liar's Hour.

"Pretty well," answered Jim, "Gary had the best day—25 fish."

"And only one five-pounder," Gary said, smiling broadly.

Few fishermen hook and land more than eight rainbows at Lower Talarik Creek during a full day's fishing—25 sounded too good to be true. But Gary was smiling all night. Not surprisingly, two days later they wanted to return to the creek; this time I took them.

Jim and Bart went upstream a few hundred yards to the spot they'd fished before, leaving Gary to fish the Rock Hole. This was a straight stretch 200 yards long and perhaps 60 feet wide, so named for a large rock lying near the west bank. A good fly-fisherman can cast the width of the stream with ease, although today a 15-knot upstream breeze made it more difficult. The almost clear creek water varied in depth from one to three feet, flowing fairly smoothly over a graveled bottom toward a small pond immediately downstream. Being right-handed, Gary stood on the east bank to make casting easier.

I sat on the opposite shore and watched Gary for half an hour. He was using a small salmon egg imitation, drifting it along the bottom to imitate the real thing. Although there were no longer any salmon left in the creek, spawning activity had been heavy the previous month. Eggs, frequently dislodged from the gravel bed, drifted downstream and were fair game for rainbow and grayling.

During the half hour, Gary hooked three large fish in the 10-pound class, losing one but landing the others downstream in the pond.

"Come on over and give it a try," Gary called, releasing a beautiful 10-pounder in the pond. "There's plenty for all."

I didn't need any further encouragement. Taking my own flyrod out of its case, I assembled it and waded across the stream to where he'd just hooked another fish.

"Cast right over there," my client-turned-guide called out. "You can't miss."

He was right. For the next hour, Gary and I changed places eight times, taking turns hooking rainbows and working them downstream to release them in the pond while the other walked back up and did it again. It was a merry-go-round of rainbow trout fishing—but it took a master fisherman to do it. Those fish didn't get to be 10 pounds by foolishly striking every lure presented to them. After an hour, I had to acknowledge that maybe Gary did land 25 fish the last time.

But Lower Talarik Creek was in danger; while the State of Alaska had already designated other streams in the area fly-fishing-only, this stream remained open to the use of spinners. Very few fish were being taken home by the numerous fly-fishermen each year, but the spin fishermen almost invariably killed their catch. I could foresee the day when the fish declined in both size and numbers to the point where they would ultimately disappear entirely. Something had to be done to preserve this resource.

Earlier that September, I'd met a fish biologist from the Alaska Department of Fish and Game on the creek. Lew Gwartney, assigned to the King Salmon office, was making his rounds of the area, particularly to see how the creek was responding to the increased fishing pressure. I'd spoken to Lew about this problem before but Lew felt that Alaskan streams should be open to all kinds of fishermen regardless of what kind of tackle they used. Not only wouldn't he support my idea of reserving the stream for fly-fishing-only—if he had his way, all the waters now restricted would be opened back up again to spinners and treble hooks. I disagreed, of course, and continued to push my own idea of trying to conserve what we had before it was lost.

The argument isn't over the type of tackle used, but the type of people who use it. There's no question in my mind that fly-fishermen are definitely more conservation-minded than other kinds—not because they fish with a flyrod but because most of the people who fish with a flyrod are gentler with the fish they catch. By carefully handling each trout and salmon, these benevolent anglers make sure the fish they release have the best chance for survival. I've seen too many spin fishermen drop-kick fish back into the stream to agree that the resource should be kept open to all fishing methods. That approach has already destroyed most of the trout and salmon streams in the Lower 48.

Having gotten nowhere with the Department of Fish and Game, my next step was to appeal to the Alaska Board of Fisheries, the panel empowered with setting rules for all fishing within the state. I submitted a written proposal to declare this lovely but vulnerable tundra stream fly-fishing-only, and decided to appear when the Board met in open session in Anchorage during December.

I thought I'd have a better chance if other sport fishermen spoke for my proposal, so I asked George Dickson, an Anchorage attorney, and Roger Moore, president of Security National Bank in Anchorage to testify. Both of these men were ardent fly-fishermen who'd been with me on the creek that fall and agreed whole-heartedly with my position. Although busy men themselves, each took time to attend the hearing, wait hours as the board considered other proposals, and then speak strongly in support of mine.

In a vote of four to three, the board approved our proposal and, starting with the 1981 season, Lower Talarik Creek has been restricted to fly-fishing only. Although fishing pressure hasn't dropped a great deal, the significant change has been the small numbers of fish actually killed. Catch-and-release is gaining support, particularly among fly-fishermen, and we now look forward to a fall run of large rainbow trout in Lower Talarik Creek indefinitely.

CHAPTER 34

I t's one thing to be skunked when you're out by yourself; it's quite another when you're guided to it by a so-called expert—the so-called expert being, in this case, myself when I first started fishing for arctic char in Iliamna.

Experience isn't only the best teacher; in the guiding business, it's the only teacher. Unfortunately, when we started out in the Spring of 1977, I may have been bursting with enthusiasm and eager to please, but I didn't know much about the local fishing streams.

Losing our first plane on the Mulchatna left me a little leery about landing our precious aircraft in places where I'd never been before. On the other hand, how else were we to find the good fishing spots? If I stopped exploring, we'd be forced to fish only a few of the better-known streams—and they were already becoming crowded during peak fishing periods. Explore I must—as I quickly learned with our first fishing guests.

Dick and Shirley Follett of Anchorage had visited the lodge a year before we took over, fishing the Newhalen River during the sockeye salmon run in July. They returned with their son Vince in early June of our first season to go after some rainbow trout and arctic char.

Before the Wilders moved out, Dave left with me a list of fishing streams in the area. The Iliamna River was included on this list with the notation "arctic char." So, although I'd never

185

fished the stream myself, I decided to take the Folletts there.

Mary had an appointment in Anchorage to see her doctor so I dropped Dick, Shirley, and Vince off at the mouth of the river, returned to the lodge to pick up Mary, and flew on to Anchorage, planning to return in the afternoon to pick up the Folletts. At least the weather was nice.

When I got back, I found their fishing had been terrible. They'd caught only one char near the river mouth and, when they'd tried to walk upstream along the bank to find some better fishing (as I'd suggested that morning), they discovered that I'd left them on an island and the water was too deep for them to cross the stream, even in hip boots—they ended up standing around a campfire much of the day.

What a blunder—and with our first fly-out guests at that. Extremely embarrassed, I suggested stopping off on the way home at another river where I thought we'd find better fishing. But I hadn't fished the new river either, and once more my clients were skunked. To top it all off, we spent so much time looking for fish that by the time we returned to the lodge, we'd missed supper and had to eat leftovers.

The next week, on a calm day with the lake surface mirror-smooth, I had my son Bill run our 14' Jon boat with a 9-1/2 horsepower outboard 35 miles up the lake to the mouth of the Iliamna River. Bill was waiting on the beach when I arrived in the Cessna, and we pulled the boat high and dry, tying it securely to a tree before returning to the lodge. A week after that, I took all three boys back to the river to begin exploring further upstream in the boat. We had to find out if there were enough fish there to justify sending any more guests after them.

The river is wide and slow-moving at the mouth, having formed a series of channels in the sandy bottom land of the valley. As we left the delta, the trees closed in on both sides of the stream, the dark green 40-foot tall spruces clearly dominating in number the lighter green of the 50-foot cottonwoods and shorter clumps of alder. Scouler and feltleaf willow flourished under the canopy of spruce and cottonwood, their tops chewed down to snow level by hungry moose during the winter months. The clear water had a trace of blue in the deeper pools, hinting of an origin among the snow-packed mountains to the northeast.

The river meanders through the steeply-sided valley twisting and turning like a snake, creating shallow gravel bars on the inside of each turn and eroding the outside so deeply that the roots of the trees growing close to the winding river were undercut and exposed. Many had toppled into the stream, their massive root structures still holding firm to the shore while their branches and trunks formed long sweepers pointing toward the center of the stream. As we moved slowly upriver, the stream bed gradually turned from sand to gravel, the gravel becoming coarser the farther we went. So far in our journey we hadn't seen any fish.

A few miles from the mouth, we found a smaller stream entering the river from the southeast. We stopped to try a cast or two into the confluence and Tommy's small Mepps spinner had moved only a foot or two underwater before a two-foot-long silver streak nailed it in mid-current. We were fast into our first char. I hadn't yet been able to convince my sons of the joys of fly-fishing.

Unlimbering my own rod, I tied on a small streamer and laid a cast well out into the current. Twitching the weighted fly as it slowly sank from view, I saw another silver char dart up from the sandy bottom and take the feathered morsel. "Reel in, boys," I called, fighting the fish to the side of the boat. "We know they're here and what they'll hit. Let's move upstream."

"But Dad, this is great fishing here," came a chorus of complaints from the boys. They'd all landed fish by this time.

"That's not the point, boys," I said. "A guide has to know the whole river, not just a few holes. Before we can take any more guests here we have to know if there are any more good holes, where they are, and how to fish them. This could be the only good fishing hole on the river, or it could be only one of many. We've got a lot of exploring to do today."

Several miles upstream we found the first big hole. Well over a hundred char darted about in the crystalline backwater out of the main current. Why there were fish here and not in any of the other places we'd stopped to look was still a mystery. But at least now we'd started learning where to look. That night we tied the

boat to a log on an island near the mouth of the river and flew
back to Iliamna, eager to report our success to a doubting Mary.

A few days later, when I was flying to Pile Bay at the eastern
end of Lake Iliamna, I decided to check on the boat. It was gone—
not only the boat itself but also the log to which it had been tied.
It took several more passes before I spotted it, overturned and
partially submerged, lodged firmly among several uprooted
trees jammed against the shore. Apparently, heavy rains since
our last visit had created a flood that had swept it away.
Fortunately, we'd removed the motor.

The next day the boys and I flew back to retrieve the boat and
move it upstream a few miles. The water had risen at least six
feet along the river, sweeping away much of the debris we'd seen
there before. Unlike many other streams within the Iliamna
area, which flow through smaller lakes that dampen the effects
of heavy rains, this particular river flows directly out of the
mountains. So that was what those deeply undercut banks were
trying to tell me!

We started taking guests to fish the river shortly thereafter
and quickly learned that our initial success with Mepps spinners and streamer patterns wouldn't always be repeated. The
arctic char—cousin to the eastern brook trout, lake trout, and
Dolly Varden of the West Coast—proved to be quite fussy at
times.

It was Tom, bitten by the fly-fishing bug by then, who discovered the first of our standby flies on one of his trips. Mary went
along on that particular trip, taking a day off in early August.
We'd so regaled her with stories of the beauty of the river and the
abundance of fish that when the opportunity came to try it
herself, she leapt at the chance. When they arrived, however,
recent rains had again raised the water level three feet above
normal and, instead of being able to fish the main stream, the
group had had to fish close to the banks to avoid the heavy
current. The char, wise to the heavy water, also sought the ed-
dies, both for food and to save energy.

By noon, and still fishless, Mary had worked her way through
the brush along the high outside bank to an eddy in an old channel. The pocket of slack water was only 30 feet long by 15 to 20

feet wide, with a fallen spruce partially blocking the outlet to the river. Several feet deep, the pool provided just the kind of cover the char were looking for, and Mary spotted a beauty in the clear water almost directly beneath her. With a short line and some very careful casting around branches, she laid the fly within sight of the fish and twitched it a few times. The fish rose to the bait with a lunge.

Mary squealed with delight, bringing Tom racing up the bank to watch Mary and the thrashing char wage tug-o-war in the back water, the strong fish valiantly trying for the open current and Mary just as determined to contain it on her light flyrod. With only a few feet to work in and branches and roots in every direction, it was a wild contest, the char fiercely challenging Mary for its freedom. On top of that, there was nowhere to safely land it.

Tom finally corralled it next to the bank and flipped it up among the brush. At 27 inches long and 7 pounds in weight, it was the largest char taken so far that season. Mary was one proud lady in the lodge that night.

Equally important, the fly she'd used was the popular West Coast steelhead pattern called a Polar Shrimp. When tied on a #6 hook, this fly seldom fails to produce at least a few fish each day.

We continued to fish the river during the remainder of the first season and on into 1978, always experimenting with new patterns on the wary char. Tom started taking fish fairly regularly on a Black Wooly Worm, while I found the Polar Shrimp and Ted's Yesterday the most successful. My own design was a streamer pattern tied to imitate the salmon and char smolt born within the river system. Salmon egg imitations started working in mid-August as the hordes of sockeye salmon started spawning, but the most unusual pattern we discovered came about almost by accident during our second season.

Tom had been guiding two fly-fisherman from San Francisco, Bob Friese and Dick Carpeneti, one day in early September; when they returned to the lodge that night, he immediately sought me out.

"Dad, do we have anything that will imitate a maggot?"

"What do you mean by a maggot?"

"You know. A MAGGOT. A small white worm. There are zillions of them up there, coming out of those dead salmon carcasses along the shore. The char are gobbling them up like candy."

"How do you know they're eating the maggots?" I asked.

"I checked the stomach on the char we ate for lunch," Tom answered. "Believe it or not, the back half was full of salmon eggs and the front half packed full of maggots. The fish had switched from eggs to maggots sometime last night or this morning, and just kept on feeding. It was really stuffed with them."

I took Tom over to our box of flies and opened it to a group of drys. "We can try clipping the wings and hackle off a #12 Light Cahill," I suggested. "The cream body looks almost like a maggot, and it should float for awhile if you grease it well with floatant. Try it next time you go."

It was a few days before Tom had a chance to try his new idea out on the char. "No good, Dad," he said as soon as he'd returned. "They wouldn't even go near it. We tried it several times, both wet and dry, and finally had to go back to the Egg Fly and Polar Shrimp."

"What was the water like?" I asked.

"Way down. Hasn't rained up there in a week."

"That must be it, then," I said. Apparently, everything had to be just right for the maggot hatch to work. The salmon start upstream in mid-July but don't spawn until August. And then they don't all spawn at once but stretch it out over eight to ten weeks, so for two months there are fish spawning along the whole stream. Then they die, wash up on the shore, and start to rot—and incidentally creating that putrid smell common to our salmon rivers. Then the flies come along and lay their eggs on the rotting carcasses.

The weather is usually nice in August, with little rain; the river would therefore remain at low water. When the fly eggs hatch, the maggots live on the dead salmon; then it rains again, and the stream level starts to rise and cover the salmon carcasses. The maggots wash away in the current and the char start to feed on this easy-to-catch food, no longer having to fight the salmon for their eggs.

"Next year, Tom," I said, "we'll try it again with a new maggot pattern."

It doesn't look like much—we took a #12 dry fly hook and tightly wound white deer body hair from eye to bend, clipping the hair very short to about the size of a maggot. It's a time-consuming tying process, but the buoyant deer hair floats very well and looks like the real thing when floating down the river. The char love it—and so do the trout.

In spring and early summer, the primary food of the arctic char is salmon fry hatched from the past summer's spawn. They also feed on year-old fry, called smolt, or young salmon that already have survived their first full year in fresh water. Fly-tying books are full of smolt imitations but remarkably deficient when it comes to patterns tied to look like the little fry, fish only an inch or so long. My own Ted's Yesterday is a reasonable smolt imitation, but one day I decided to get more basic and develop a fry look-alike. My newest creative attempt of hair and feathers is as follows:

Hook - #8 or #10, average length, such as single salmon 36890 or 9671

Tail - tan hackle fibers, sparse

Body - white wool, wound tight

Neck - tan hackle fibers, sparse

Wing - white kip tail

Head - black tying silk, small

It's basically a small white streamer but more like the actual fish than other fancier patterns. I gave it to David to field test one day in late spring when he was guiding on the char river. I had a pretty good idea it would work on the char because I'd already tried it successfully on some Dolly Varden on Kodiak Island.

"What do you call this thing, Dad?" David wanted to know.

"Haven't given it a name yet. Let me know how you like it."

Dave came home that evening radiant with enthusiasm over the new fly. "There's nothing to it, Dad," he raved. "Remember how we sometimes used to fish all day up there, and watched the char swim away from our flies? This is just the opposite. We cast it close and they rush to take it, almost as fast as the rainbows. Makes the guide look like he knows what he's doing for a change on those stubborn char. There's really nothing to it."

And so we now call it the Nothing fly. Simple to tie and deadly on the char, it looks like the best fry imitation yet—although we'll keep on experimenting, of course.

Chapter 35

Winter passed quickly that year. Liz and Angie were attending the local public school; Tom had completed his aircraft mechanic's course and was enrolled in flight school in Tacoma, Washington; David was a high school senior in Kodiak. Bill had left school to manage a cable TV station in Skagway.

The lodge was still open for business, keeping Mary and me busy. Between seeing to the guests, we spent a lot of time discussing our future and planning our annual winter trip Outside. (To an Alaskan, Outside refers to the other 49 states.)

Since our association with Alaska Outdoors was over, we had to expand our own advertising. Being somewhat familiar with the sportsmans-show routine, we signed up for the International Sportsmen's Exposition opening in San Mateo, California on February 20th, and the World Outdoor Exposition opening in Suffern, New York a week later.

I'd also committed myself to presenting an evening program to four different fly-fishing clubs on the West Coast, so while tying flies that fall and winter, I brushed up on my Robert Service poetry, committing two more poems to memory. My repertoire now included six pieces: the perennial favorites, *The Shooting of Dan McGrew* and *The Cremation of Sam McGee*, plus the deeply moving *Spell of the Yukon* as well as three others, *Ballad of the Iceworm Cocktail, The Ballad of Blasphemous Bill,* and *The Ballad of Salvation Bill.* With these I could entertain a

group for an hour without repeating myself. I used the tapes I'd
made with Jim for the fishing part of each program—although
several in attendance at each meeting said that the poetry was
more entertaining.

Before we could go anywhere, however, I had to balance the
books for the year. My office was the larger of two dining room
tables, within reach of both the telephone and the filing cabinet;
Mary had her sewing machine on the other, working on a new
dress for Liz.

I finished up the month of December and computed the final
balance for 1979.

"Mary," I said, staring at the figures in incredulity, "you're not
going to believe this."

"What?" she asked, turning off the machine.

"The lodge actually made a profit in 1979."

"You're kidding." Mary got up to see for herself. "How much?"

"Almost $10,000."

Mary started to laugh. "Considering the hours we put in this
year, Ted, I figure that means we made about five cents an hour.
Isn't there a law?"

"Unfortunately," I said, "about a third of it came from drop-
ins."

The lodge couldn't support itself on fishing alone, but at least
we were finally making some progress. I knew Mary was looking
forward to the day when we could close for the winter. Maybe
next year.

We left Iliamna on Sunday, January 13th in the Cessna 206
I'd bought in August. David took a commercial flight from
Kodiak and met us in Anchorage, and Bill joined us in White-
horse, Yukon Territory. He'd taken the narrow-gauge railway
up from Skagway. We were pretty crowded with all six of us in
the plane plus luggage, supplies for the shows, and half a moose
hide I'd promised to Buz's Fly Shop in California. Mary and I sat
up front, with Bill and David in the middle seats; the back seats
were piled high with cargo and Liz and Angie sprawled on the
moose hide.

Tom met us at the Tacoma airport in his new Volkswagon and
drove Mary and me to a hotel with the girls. Bill and Dave stayed

with Tom at his one-bedroom apartment, sleeping on a mattress on his living-dining room floor. On Sunday, while Mary and the girls went shopping, the three boys and I watched the Superbowl on Tom's TV. Halfway through the game, the phone rang.

"Dad, it's for you," Tom said, calling me to the phone. "It's Scott." Scott Bauer was lodge sitting in Iliamna. "He's got some bad news."

A windstorm with velocities reaching 100 knots had blown down the small metal building we'd built over the generator last September. The generator itself wasn't damaged, and Scott had put up a temporary shelter of plywood to protect the engine and electrical windings, but the hangar was more difficult to repair. The wind had blown the hangar doors inward; when that happened the west wall exploded outward, scattering wood splinters clear to Roadhouse Bay. The roof and other two walls were still standing, but it was his opinion that one more storm like that would finish the job. He said he'd try to strengthen the structure as best he could, but the storm had also dumped two feet of snow on the area.

"Look on the bright side, Dad," Tom said. "At least the 206 is down here."

"Maybe you're right, Tom." I said. "Scott said they dragged the floats out of the hangar in case the rest of it falls over."

"Then we'll be flying two planes again this summer for sure," he added, anxious to start flying at the lodge. "I should have my seaplane rating by then."

Mary, the girls, and I left the next day for the Baja Peninsula. It was a place I'd always wanted to go, and Mary readily agreed to the trip for our vacation that winter. We flew the length of the peninsula, down the East Coast along the Gulf of California all the way to Cabo San Lucas, and back up the Pacific Ocean side. We stayed at the local hotels and ate their seafood specialties each night, where Mary frequently inquired into the ingredients they'd used. The flying weather was clear and calm for the entire trip south of the border. After two weeks we flew back to Los Angeles and stayed with Mary's sister Jean and her husband Jack, who'd moved to Ventura.

For another week we enjoyed the Southern California winter

weather. In the evenings I drove into L.A. for three of the fly-fishing club meetings I'd agreed to address. On February 15th, I flew over the range of mountains that separates the Los Angeles basin from the San Joaquin Valley to speak at a meeting in Visalia. Mickey Powell of Buz's Fly Shop had arranged a dinner meeting of fly-fishermen in his area.

I stayed with Mickey and his family that night, and the next morning he drove me to the airport where I called for a weather briefing. After listening to the weather report, I turned to Mickey. "I may be back tonight. They're reporting low clouds, wind, and rain between here and Ventura."

The weather at Visalia was sunny and mild, although a brisk 15-knot breeze from the north had sprung up overnight. I started experiencing some light turbulence immediately after take-off; at my cruising altitude of 3,000 feet it became moderate at times, throwing the light airplane up, down, and sideways as I churned my way south. Over Bakersfield I called for the latest weather from the Flight Service Station—it was not good, and deteriorating. "I must caution you that VFR flight is not recommended," the controller said.

"I'll take a look at the pass and give you a pilot report," I said, and continued south.

By the time I reached the height of land in the pass between Bakersfield and Los Angeles, the turbulence had become more uncomfortable, straining my seatbelt in the downdrafts. Rain had reduced my visibility to less than five miles, and I had to alter course frequently to avoid the clouds building along the route.

Peering ahead through the rain-swept windshield, I could see a solid barrier of coal-black clouds joined together from the murky overcast above me to the hills below. Heavy rain soon started hammering at the airplane, so hard I could hear it over the roar of the engine—with visibility reduced to less than a mile, I turned back toward Visalia. I called Mickey from the airport and he came out to pick me up.

Mickey and his family live in a four-bedroom, two-bath house in a quiet, suburban neighborhood. Two of their four children still lived at home and joined Mickey, his wife, and me at the table that evening. We'd just finished dinner when Mickey called me to the phone. "It's Mary, Ted," he said, handing me the kitchen phone and quickly leaving the room.

"Hi, Mary," I said. "I tried to get back but the passes were all closed by the storm. You weren't worried, were you?"

"No, I'm all right," she said, but her voice trembled. "Did Scott call you from the lodge yet?"

"No, why should he? What's happened now? The rest of the hangar, I suppose."

Mary's voice faltered. "There's been an accident, Ted. Tom was in an airplane crash."

"Was anybody hurt?" I asked. Since I'd survived two crashes myself, I hardly expected anything serious.

"Tom was killed," Mary said. "He was flying two friends down to Reno and flew into some bad weather in the mountains north of Redding. Everybody died. It happened yesterday."

Chapter 36

Somehow we got through the rest of the winter. Tom was buried on the East Coast in his mother's family plot. We got back to Alaska to find the hangar still standing—but it didn't seem very important any more.

Ironically, the start of our 1980 season was the best ever, with reasonably good flying weather and plenty of clients to keep us busy. Kaufmann's Fly Shop in Portland had run a two-page spread about us in their annual winter catalog and 15 of their fly-fishing clients had called to book space at the lodge that season. When added to the reservations we already had, we were now 30% booked for the coming season—and well over half of them were fly-fishermen.

Both Bill and David returned as guides that summer. We had to hire another, Guy Smith, from Kenai to take Tom's place. Reuben Dunagan was unable to return so we hired Randy Yeager from Anchorage to take over as second pilot. Mary's mother, Martha Wickersham, offered to help with the cooking.

Our choice of staff turned out to be excellent, and the season went so well both Mary and I marvelled at how smoothly the lodge could operate. Our experience was finally starting to pay off, and that spring I traded the old 180 for another 206.

Mary started each day at 5:00 a.m. Although we'd hired another cook each summer, she still preferred to fix breakfast herself, rising early to get everything ready. Mary is definitely a morning person.

I'd usually steal another 10 to 15 minutes in bed before getting up to wake the guests at 5:30. During their first few days in camp, many guests would get to the morning coffee pot before me, unwilling to waste a minute, but by the third or fourth morning, they became harder to wake up. Instead of a cheery good morning when I knocked, I got groans, grunts and even, occasionally, a few unkind words. But everyone knew the planes left at 7:00 for the fishing grounds.

The next thing was to check the weather forecast and decide whether or not we would, indeed, fly that day. The chief weather forecaster—or dart thrower, as we called him—for all of Alaska had visited us once during our second year at the lodge. According to him, his forecast accuracy usually depended on how good the weather was. The nicer the weather, the more reliable the forecast—and vice versa.

To a pilot, it's the vice versa that counts. Almost anyone can fly safely in fair weather—it's the foul that causes problems. Fog, wind, rain, snow—the worse it got, the worse his forecasts. So it was up to those of us in the business of flying to draw on our own experience and local knowledge before deciding to fly that day—and then worry until all the planes have safely landed again.

Breakfast was usually over by 6:30. While the guests returned to their rooms to prepare for the day, Randy and I started the daily routine of thoroughly checking the aircraft, including pumping out each individual float compartment to check for water seepage, checking oil and fuel for both quantity and possible contamination, and cleaning the windshield.

We made a performance check of the engine while taxiing before the first take-off each day: Oil and fuel pressure normal; cylinder head temperature in the green; electrical charge from the generator; vacuum for instrument operation; magneto check; cycle the propellor; controls free; flaps working; gyros operational and compass set; altimeter set to lake elevation; doors and windows locked; radios on and working properly; seat belts fastened.

With all guests aboard plus lunch and fishing tackle, fuel for outboards, rafts if needed, and the ever-present emergency equipment kit, we were usually airborne by 7:00 AM. Since I was normally both guide and pilot on those all-day excursions, the lodge was in Mary's hands until 6:00 that evening.

Mary planned all the menus, selecting the recipes and ordering all the food for guests and staff. She monitored the housekeeping and did most of the baking herself, as well as preparing lunch for the crew. Although another cook prepared the evening meal, Mary was always on hand to help and advise. It is Mary's goal to correct problems before they can escalate into trouble for the guests.

So while Mary struggled to keep the lodge running smoothly, I did the same out on the streams with the day's fishing. So many different things could affect whether our guests caught the fish they wanted that even now, after years of guiding, I can't always predict the results. Weather always has an impact—but not as much as the individual skills of the fishermen themselves and how well they listen to advice. In most streams, the sport fish are concentrated in holding water; sometimes near the bank, sometimes nearer mid-stream, and sometimes evenly distributed across the entire creek. Too often a guest would wade right into the holding water I'd just pointed out and start casting past it toward the opposite shore.

"You're standing where you should be fishing," I'd say almost weekly to one angler or another.

One thing I learned never to do: tell another fly-fisherman that the particular pattern he'd selected wouldn't catch fish. I did that once—and then watched one particularly stubborn guest fish his own fly for two hours just to prove me wrong. He finally did catch a fish on it, but he might have taken a dozen on the pattern I'd recommended.

The accomplished fly-fisherman is a pleasure to guide and makes my job as easy as it is satisfying. The beginner, on the other hand, presents the greater challenge—and the beginner who thinks himself an expert perhaps the greatest challenge of all.

I remember once we were fishing the Brooks River, a two-mile-long stream flowing from Brooks Lake to Naknek Lake within Katmai National Park. I had two English couples with me, Mount and Daphne Conyngham, a delightful pair who'd been with me before, and their friends, John and Judith Shirley, a dour and straight-laced couple in their mid-50's on their first trip to Alaska. I'd taken them to the Brooks River because I knew it was full of migrating sockeye salmon, fresh from Bristol Bay.

Mount was an expert with the flyrod, hooking one fish after another all day long. Daphne and John weren't in his class but, with some careful planning of beats, I managed to get each of them into several fish. But despite all my efforts, Judith caught no fish all morning.

Her casting barely reached 20 feet. She was standing on a shallow gravel bar near the middle of the stream, and I could see the gray shapes of hundreds of salmon swimming in an arc around her position. The fish passed just a few feet beyond her casts.

I must have waded out to her half a dozen times that morning to show her how to cast. Each time she very patiently listened, watched my demonstration, and promised to do better. But as I returned to the shore each time and looked around, I could see she'd immediately returned to her old ways.

After lunch Judith continued to cast short. She was back out on the same gravel bar she'd fished all morning. The deeper water was directly in front of her; schools of salmon were slowly moving past heading upstream 30 feet away in the deeper water. As I approached, she patiently turned around and assumed that classic pose: "Here he comes again. Humor the poor man. Be nice, but don't listen. After all, we English have been fly-fishing much longer than these colonials."

I stopped a few feet away and said very sweetly, "Judith, where you are fishing there are no fish. They are all circling ten feet beyond your cast." Then I turned and walked ashore.

When I reached the bank, Judith was still watching me. Wire-framed glasses outlined her furrowed eyebrows as she stared at me in perplexity. I waved and turned to one of the others in the party.

Out of the corners of my eyes I watched her turn back to the river and resume fishing. But now, her casting had so miraculously improved that she was easily reaching the school of migrating salmon. She hooked a nice fish—and finally smiled.

All parties were usually back at the lodge by 6:30 each evening—just in time for Liars' Hour before dinner began at 7:30. I paid close attention to each guest's story since, through them, I remained current on stream conditions throughout the area. After dinner—and after conferring with the other guides—I made the fishing assignments for the next day, advising each person where they were going to fish and what kind of flies the fish would probably be taking. By 10:00 just about everybody was in bed and asleep, including Mary and me.

CHAPTER 37

Most of our clients that year were fly-fishermen; unfortunately some were not. Late one night in June, Mary and I woke up to the insistent ringing of the telephone in our bedroom.

"Iliaska Lodge," I answered.

"Where the hell have you been?" snarled a man's voice. "You bastards were supposed to pick us up at the goddam airport!"

"Who is this?" I demanded, suddenly wide awake. "Are you sure you have the right number?"

"Hell yes, I got the right number, buddy. This is Joe Smith from Nebraska."

Mary was sitting up by then. Joe was shouting so loudly I was holding the earpiece a foot from my ear, and she could hear every word. "There's a Joe Smith party due in tomorrow for a three-day package," she whispered. "I remember them being from Nebraska."

"You are expected here tomorrow, Mr. Smith," I told him. "Where are you calling from?"

"Anchorage, you SOB! Where do you think?"

"If you'll check the letter I sent confirming your reservations, you'll find that I said we would meet you at the Iliamna airport—not in Anchorage. Go back to the Anchorage airport tomorrow morning and take a commercial flight to Iliamna. We'll meet you here."

"See you in hell, you lying bastard!" Joe shouted, and hung up. I turned over to go back to sleep but found I was so mad I couldn't get my eyelids to stay shut. "What hotel did he say they were staying in?" I asked Mary. "We don't have to put up with the likes of him. I'm going to call him back and cancel his reservations."

"He didn't say," she said. "Maybe they'll be all right when they sober up."

Joe called back in the morning, sober and contrite, and the trio arrived on the afternoon flight. I was out flying all day, and by the time I got back, they'd begun drinking again. Joe was the leader of the group, a short, balding, red-faced man of about 60. He was a banker by profession, business partner and financier of the other two fishermen, George Ball and Richard Nobbins. George was the taller, a lean, rough construction company owner in his 40s. Richard, older and quieter than either of the other two, was George's foreman.

Over dinner, I explained our policy of catch-and-release as I do with all newcomers. All three of them were seated at my end of the table—Mary was at the other end talking to guests who'd been with us a few days already, trying to keep their attention away from Joe's group.

"We came here to catch fish," Joe said. "Naturally we want to take some home."

"You can take as many salmon as the State of Alaska allows," I said. "But the char, rainbows, and grayling have to be released."

"I don't see why," Joe argued. "We're only here for a few days. What difference can it make?"

"If everybody kills all the fish they catch, we'll soon be fished out—and then there won't be any fish for anybody."

"What are you worrying about?" Joe said, pushing back his chair to get up for seconds. "It'll be good fishing up here for years. Look at Canada. Our last trip up there we brought 1500 pounds of fish back with us. If they don't worry about overfishing, why should you?"

"Maybe they should," I said.

The following morning Joe and his group went with Randy

to a char river while I took another group rainbow fishing. When we returned in the evening Randy was upset. "I couldn't watch them all at once, Ted. Joe was fishing around a bend from the other two and killed several fish before I got back to check on him. Then George killed a few when I was gone."

"I was afraid this might happen," I said. "I gave them my usual lecture last night, but I could see it wasn't going over. Were they spin-fishing or fly-fishing?"

"All spinners," he answered. "They even started with treble hooks. I had to check each time they changed lures to see that they obeyed the law and cut two hooks off."

"How many fish did you bring back?"

"Almost a dozen—all four- to five-pounders," he answered. "This is the first day I haven't enjoyed myself on the river."

"Well, my guess is they would have killed a lot more if you hadn't been there to stop most of it," I said. "Go get something to eat—I'll take them tomorrow."

The next day I took them to the Nushagak River, the next major drainage west of Iliamna. There were no restrictions on size or type of fishing equipment on the Nushagak, and each of the guests brought their stoutest rods and heaviest lines and lures. Each of them hooked and landed several king and chum salmon apiece, skidding them up onto the shallow gravel beach and clubbing each on its head to kill it. We never reached the limit of five fish apiece so I didn't have to worry about how they would react to releasing salmon. Each laughed and joked all day, their enjoyment reinforced regularly from the case of beer they'd insisted on bringing along. We brought back 12 fish for them to take to Nebraska.

At breakfast on their last day, Joe asked where they were fishing that morning. Since their flight left Iliamna in the afternoon, they were entitled to a boat and guide for the morning.

"The Newhalen River," I said. "There are plenty of rainbow trout and grayling there, plus a few char. You should get plenty of action."

"What about keeping some fish?"

"Not there."

"If we can't kill fish, there's no sense fishing," Joe decided.

"We're not going."

"It's up to you," I said. "But if you change your mind, the guide and boat will be ready."

Joe and his friends sat at the table, drank coffee laced with bourbon, and played cards all morning. After lunch, they packed their things, took their frozen fish, and left.

"You were right," Mary said that evening when I returned from flying. "We should have found out where they were staying and called them back that night and cancelled their reservations. What an unpleasant group of people."

About a month later we received a letter from the Commissioner of Fish and Game asking for information about Joe Smith. Joe had written to the Department complaining about our lodge operation and our restrictive catch-and-release policy—he even accused us of overcharging him.

I wrote back describing their stay and their refusal to respect our catch-and-release policy. A month later the commissioner sent us a copy of his answer to Joe, which stated in expanded bureaucratic jargon, of course, that if Joe felt he had a legitimate complaint, he could seek redress in the civil courts, but that the department fully supported the conservation efforts of Alaska's more reputable guides and outfitters.

We never heard from Joe again and that fall we decided that, from now on, we'd accept only fly-fishermen.

CHAPTER 38

T he Copper River flows westward out of the mountains
separating Lake Iliamna from Lower Cook Inlet and
Kamishak Bay. This beautiful stream combines Alaskan wilderness with the fighting courage of the world-famous
Iliamna rainbow trout. Starting in hundreds of snow-laden
gullies and ravines tucked into the upper slopes, the water
trickles and splashes downhill over ledge and gravel into a
system of small lakes interconnected by a gently flowing
stream.

Four miles below the final lake in the chain, the river
plunges over a 40-foot waterfall. Stands of tall spruce grow in
the floor of the valley, trailing thinly up some of the ridges
toward the circling hills. Water-seeking cottonwoods line the
river banks, their shallow taproots assured of an ample supply
of the precious liquid throughout the year. Alder, stunted
birch, willow, smaller shrubs, and grasses add to the mix of
vegetation.

The river meanders as all good trout water should, offering
a variety of pools, runs, undercut banks, and gravel bars to
interest even the most discerning of fly-fishermen. When
everything is right, the river teems with rainbows; it has been
called the finest trout stream in the world.

In our early years, I often took clients along on reconnais-
sance trips; on one of my first visits to the Copper River, I

brought along Ken and Barb Holland from California. Ken and Barb were experienced fly-fishermen, having fished primarily in Montana and Idaho. A couple in their 40s, they enjoyed fishing together and were a delightful pair of dinner guests each evening.

The day in early August was simply beautiful: temperatures between 65 and 70 degrees, light breezes, sunshine—and no bugs to speak of. The gravel stream bed was covered with pairs of sockeye salmon starting their spawning ritual; although the actual egg-laying had barely started, the trout were already hovering around the pending feast, ravenously hungry.

The fly I'd recommended was, therefore, an egg pattern that imitated the salmon egg. But Ken and Barb were dry-fly enthusiasts and refused all my suggestions to match-the-hatch and try an egg pattern.

"We didn't come all this way to fish with lead along the bottom," Ken said. "We prefer to fish dry."

"You wouldn't mind if I try it with an egg?" I asked.

"Go right ahead. There appears to be enough for all."

I put an egg on and was taking a strike almost every cast, while Ken and Barb worked their dry flies over fish oblivious to everything but eggs. They eventually took a few smaller trout, all less than a pound, and, by the time the afternoon shadows were beginning to stretch across the water, neither had landed a fish over 16 inches—and in Iliamna we measure our catch in feet, not inches.

To conclude a day's fishing, I often let the boat slowly drift downstream to allow dry-fly fishermen to continue casting toward the bank as the boat moves slowly with the current. We frequently take fish in this way from small pockets of holding water not usually fished. Barb put her rod away to watch the scenery move past in slow motion, but Ken continued to fish as we drifted, hoping for one last trout before quitting.

An errant cast—perhaps a shift of wind—put Ken's fly into an overhanging bush along the bank and his leader snapped before I could turn the boat with the oars. Rather than tie on another tippet and fly, he also put his rod away.

We were approaching a riffle and deep run in which I'd seen

210

a fairly good fish during our trip upstream that morning, so casually handing Ken my own rod—with the egg fly still attached, of course—I suggested he drift it near the approaching cut bank ahead. He took my advice—the fly couldn't have been under water more than ten seconds before a beautiful two-foot-long rainbow savagely struck, set the hook firmly into its jaw, and came straight out of the river only five feet in front of Ken.

Barb shrieked as the trout twisted and turned in mid-air, falling back into the water and splashing her.

"Yeeeooowww!" Ken shouted, frantically trying to reel in the slack line as the fish darted under the boat, jumping again on the other side before it tore off downstream trying to shake the egg fly.

"Some guides will stop at nothing to get their sports into a good fish," he shouted, still losing line to the frantic trout. "How do you stop them?"

"Let it have all the line it wants," I said, noting that the fish had already taken out some of Ken's backing. "It'll turn eventually. I'll pull in to shore here so you can land it on that gravel bar."

The fish was 24 inches long and weighed four pounds, not particularly large for Iliamna but three pounds heavier than their largest fish taken that day. After a photograph and the release, Ken turned to me and said, "Thanks for the lesson, Ted."

Art Carlson was a dentist from Seattle, a dedicated fly-fisherman and a fun kind of guy to be with. He and his partner Bill Cleaver, both in their mid-40s, fished with us in mid-September and, with large numbers of lake-run trout already showing in the stream, we naturally scheduled a day on the Copper.

We now had a jet boat on the river. The first year I'd attended the sportsmans show in Suffern, New York, Bert Van Sciver, owner of The Bait Shop in Rowayton, Connecticut, had occupied the space directly across the aisle from me. He sold Evinrude outboard motors and I needed two 35 horsepower models. We talked about Alaskan fishing and outboard motors for five days at the show. On the last day, Bert finally said, "I can't stand it any longer. I've been watching that movie of you landing all those big fish too long—where do I sign up?"

The first motor Bert shipped to us in Alaska was used on the Copper River. At my request, Bert had installed a jet unit in place of the propellor, allowing us to operate in very shallow water without damage to the boat or motor. Bert has not only become my supplier of outboards but, having fished and hunted with me a dozen times, a good friend as well.

Art and I stood on a gravel bar that separated the river into two channels, one wide and shallow, the other deep and narrow. As I studied the water flowing along the narrow channel, the sun shot out from behind the clouds and I thought I saw the faint gray back of a large fish lurking below in the swirling water. It was just a flicker, and the sun slipped behind the clouds again before I could show it to Art.

"Listen, Art," I said, pointing out the place, "I'm pretty sure I saw a good one over there. Try casting from ten feet back on the gravel bar so you don't spook it. See if you can drop the egg fly up near the head of the run and fish it back on a dead drift like a nymph."

Art stared at the water, its grayish surface choppy from the rapids just upstream. "How can you see anything there?"

"Polaroid glasses," I said.

On his first cast Art took a solid strike from a three-pound trout. Leaping once, the fish shook the barbless hook in mid-air and escaped with a splash.

"That's not the one I saw," I said. "Good thing you lost him or it might have spooked the big one. Try again." I left his side and returned to the boat to watch.

After that first strike, Art lost his touch. For the next twenty minutes he thrashed that run to death, fishing from one end to the other and back again, until I began to wonder if I'd been seeing things.

"Are you sure you saw a fish in there?" he finally turned to ask.

"I saw something," I admitted. "Maybe you're not getting deep enough for him. Try adding a little more split shot."

After another ten minutes, Art gave up. "If you think there's

212

a fish in there," he said, "you try for him. I think you're crazy."

Did I really see that fish or not? Had that brief ray of sunshine played tricks on me, creating a shadow that wasn't a trout? Had we been standing there fishing empty water for half an hour? It was up to me to find out.

On my second cast, a full 14 pounds of rainbow trout eagerly sucked in my fly and burst full-length through the surface film. The small egg fly—identical to Art's—was firmly lodged in the joint between its upper and lower jaws.

It took me 20 minutes to land the fish. "I'll never doubt you again," Art said. "I didn't think rainbow trout ever got that big."

Randall Kaufmann and Mickey Powell of the two West Coast fly shops each fished with me that summer, Randall in early July and Mickey in August. Len Codella, president of Thomas and Thomas, a fly-fishing shop and rod maker in Turner's Falls, Massachusetts, made his first of many trips to the lodge in August. Each of these new guests spoke highly of our operation and agreed to send some of their clients north to fish with us.

Fishing the next year was also excellent, but red ink once again dominated the books because of our decision to accept only fly-fishermen. It wasn't easy to turn away business that we'd worked so hard to get just because they preferred to use spinning tackle. But Mary and I stuck to our decision despite the losses and hoped for the best.

Little did we realize that our next disaster was to come from another quarter entirely.

CHAPTER 39

In 1980, 22 million sockeye salmon escaped the nets of Bristol Bay and entered the Kvichak River headed for their spawning beds upstream. These salmon generally have a five-year cycle, returning to the river in which they were spawned four years after hatching. The 1975 escapement was 13.1 million and, consequently, the out-migration of smolt counted in the spring of 1977 much higher than average; the return of mature fish in 1980 was phenomenal. Starting in mid-June, salmon started entering the Bay in enormous schools of leaping, silver-sided, blue-backed fish.

Ordinarily, the commercial fishermen would have harvested at least half of them, but this year a price dispute between the fishermen and processors resulted in a strike that lasted for eight days at the peak of the run—while fisherman and processor alike watched millions of salmon representing hundreds of thousands of dollars swim unmolested through the Bay. When a price was finally agreed upon and everyone went back to work, over half the salmon had already escaped upriver.

The average female sockeye carries 3,000 eggs. Assuming 11 of the 22 million salmon escaping in 1980 were female, the total number of eggs in the Kvichak watershed approached 33 billion—the trout, char, and grayling had a feast. Likewise the following spring these same sport fish continued to feed heavily on the huge numbers of salmon fry moving down each stream toward Lake Iliamna and continued to gain weight; an average 24" trout weighed over five pounds in June.

But in 1981, only 1.7 million salmon escaped the nets of the commercial fishermen. The sport fish suffered—by September, the average 24" trout had lost a pound; instead of the feeding frenzy normally seen during the summer, each fish had to work harder for fewer eggs. A 24", four-pound rainbow trout is still a healthy fish, but the lack of salmon that year meant they would continue to lose weight until the following summer, since there would be fewer fry to feed on during the spring hatch. The absence of spawners in the local streams also brought a few hungry coastal grizzlies into the villages of Iliamna and Newhalen searching for food. Many of the local natives, who depended on salmon for food for the winter, complained of the lack of fish. Clearly, something had to be done.

The regulations governing all fishing within the state are established by the Alaska Board of Fisheries, with members appointed by the governor. The Board depends on the counsel and advice of the Alaska Department of Fish and Game (ADFG), where a professional staff of biologists and managers function under the auspices of a commissioner also appointed by the governor. The board also receives input from many Fish and Game Advisory Committees that represent local interests, the Lake Clark/Lake Iliamna committee representing the communities around the two lakes. Individuals can also bring proposals to the Board, as I'd done in 1979 to get Lower Talarik Creek declared fly-fishing-only.

During the fall of 1980, Scott Bauer had dropped by the lodge to suggest that I might tag along to see what was going on at the semi-annual meeting of the local advisory committee. Andrew Wassillie, the representative from our village, had left Iliamna and they needed a replacement. The meeting was held in the City Hall building in Newhalen, with the members from most of the other villages flown in by the ADFG. Somehow, before the meeting was over, Scott had gotten me elected as the new representative from Iliamna.

After my brief tenure as City Manager of Kodiak, I wasn't too keen on getting mixed up with local politics again, especially since the committee now consisted of seven native commercial or subsistence fishermen and one Caucasian sport fisherman; seven representatives who had grown up in the local area and one outsider raised in New Jersey; seven who considered sport fishing a diversion from the business of life and one who made a business of it.

But the sockeye salmon situation brought us together. At the 1981 meeting, the ADFG biologist from their office in King Salmon explained the management plan for Bristol Bay sockeye salmon and, specifically, for the Kvichak River stocks of fish. Since the sockeye salmon normally returns every five years and the cycle also peaks every five years, the ADFG plan was designed to take advantage of this pattern. Targeted returns for the Kvichak were 2 million fish for each of the first three years, 6 million for the fourth year, and 14 million for the fifth year. Since 1980 had been a peak year, the 1981 target was only 2 million and the 1982 and 1983 targets were also 2 million.

At the request of our advisory committee I addressed the Board of Fisheries at their December meeting in Anchorage about the lack of salmon during the 1981 sockeye run. A day later at the same meeting, which normally lasts for weeks, the ADFG finfish biologist assigned to Bristol Bay proposed to increase next year's escapement from 2 to 4 million fish and the board concurred. An escapement of 4 million salmon would certainly meet all our needs.

The 1982 sport fishing season opened on June 8th as always. Within a few days I could already see a dramatic change from the year before. Where the average 24" rainbow trout weighed four pounds in 1981, now it weighed only three pounds. A large run of salmon was going to be needed to restore these fish to their once superb condition.

By mid-July, it became apparent we were in deep trouble. The ADFG had estimated a return of 13 million to the Kvichak, but the actual fish count dropped all the way down to 2.6 million.

Two feet of ice had lingered on Lake Iliamna well through the month of May, and breakup was late. Water temperatures in feeder streams and the lake itself remained several degrees colder than normal and the returning salmon had delayed their entry into the Kvichak River, milling and circling around in the Bay where they fell prey to the commercial fishermen for a longer period. A greater number of fish were therefore netted—possibly as high as 90% of the run.

To make matters worse, where it would have been relatively painless to allow an escapement of 4 out of 13 million, now, with only 2.6 million to work from, the ADFG biologists immediately reduced the size of the target escapement from the 4 million agreed upon to the original 2 million fish. When the commercial fishing season opened, 1500 drift and set-netters were ready to start fishing and Bristol Bay was alive with salmon. All the other rivers, whose water temperatures had been closer to normal, had already reached their escapement goals, so the poor Kvichak fish had no chance.

Only 1.1 million salmon entered the Kvichak River that season; of these, the Copper River received few fish.

With such a devastatingly low return of salmon to Iliamna that summer, the community again suffered. Two more ravenous grizzlies, searching for food among our houses, had to be killed. The subsistence fishermen hadn't filled their winter food cache with salmon. So once again I was asked to plead our case at the winter Board of Fisheries meeting.

The members of the Alaska Board of Fisheries were six commercial fishermen against only one sport fisherman—I quickly realized the weight of our testimony was therefore insignificant when compared with that of the commercial fishing community. On top of that, the Commercial Fish Division of the ADFG continued to insist that a 2 million sockeye escapement into the Kvichak River was sufficient to sustain the run. ADFG biologists also admitted that they had opened the Bristol Bay commercial season in both 1981 and 1982 long enough to allow the harvest of 75% of the Kvichak River return regardless of escapement goals. The Board wasn't going to be of much help until I could change the opinions of the biologists and managers

218

in the Department of Fish and Game.

It was time to go to the top. As soon as I got back from Anchorage, I wrote a letter to the commissioner of the ADFG explaining that escapements of sockeye salmon into Iliamna had been below target for the past two years because the commercial fishermen had harvested 75% of the returning fish. I reminded him that the historical harvest over the last 30 years had averaged 50% by commercial fishermen and, consequently, an escapement of 50%. I urged him to consider the needs of the residents upstream as well as those of the commercial fishermen.

The commissioner responded promptly. His letter, dated January 21, 1983, stated "...with regard to escapment goals for the Kvichak River, the current optimum number of spawners is established on a biological basis, not in terms of providing a specific number of salmon for upriver subsistence and sports users."

Now I knew why I was having so much trouble getting state people to listen to our problems in Iliamna—it was ADFG policy to ignore our needs upriver!

Unaccustomed as I am to being rated a second-class citizen by anyone, I fired off another salvo. After explaining that, without salmon—their eggs, fry, smolt, and carcasses—our sport fishing industry, which brings over $12 million into Alaska from the Lake Iliamna area alone, would disappear; I went on to complain that their people didn't walk the stream banks every day as I do; they didn't observe the daily, weekly, and monthly changes in our waters as the salmon return to spawn; they didn't have to watch thin and sickly sport fish trying to live on less-than-adequate food during off-peak salmon years; they didn't see the many weakened and lice-infested rainbow trout too weak to rid themselves of these parasites. Here we have a natural salmon hatchery, I argued, perhaps the largest in the world—and it didn't cost the state a cent—yet three out of five years it's allowed to operate at a fraction of its capacity. No one would tolerate such performance from a hatchery that the State of Alaska had built.

And as for his statement about the escapement goals for the

Kvichak River being based on the current optimum number of spawners, I wrote: "It is that basic premise that I object to. Our subsistence users in the villages around the lake object to it. Sport fishermen from Alaska and, indeed, from around the world object to it. Why shouldn't subsistence and sport fishermen be considered?"

A month later, the commissioner responded. "The Kvichak River sockeye salmon escapement strategy is attempting to do two things," he wrote. "(1) increase sockeye salmon production in nonpeak cycle years so as to eliminate the 'boom-bust' characteristic of the fishery, and (2) maintain an overall five year cycle production level equivalent to recent cycles. I have directed our commercial fisheries managers to do their utmost to ensure that our escapement objectives are met in 1983, even if that means extended closures in key harvest areas. We are constantly adjusting our management philosophy to incorporate additional information and adjust to changing times and needs."

At least they were starting to think about escapements with a broader perspective. To accomplish the first objective of their strategy, the department was going to have to increase escapements during the off-peak years. They may not yet be ready to say so, but at least their thinking had started to change.

Iliamna River arctic char, 1983.

Copper River rainbow trout, June 1983. The fish were so thin and undernourished we had to fish elsewhere that year.

The author with a 14-pound healthy rainbow trout, 1979.

Uncle Bill Ryer

CHAPTER 40

The 1983 season on the Copper River was a catastrophe. The average 24" rainbow trout—when we could find them—now weighed less than two pounds. With large heads and long thin bodies, they could barely manage to flop a few times before giving up the fight. Heavy infestations of freshwater lice further weakened them. After a few trips, I was forced to abandon the stream altogether and seek better fishing elsewhere for our guests.

If any doubt remained about who controlled the fish and game managers of Bristol Bay, it was soon evident as the 1983 sockeye salmon season opened. True to their word, the department kept the commercial season closed until the escapement into the Kvichak reached almost 2 million fish—but once it opened, they kept it open almost continuously for the next four weeks. The commercial harvest in Bristol Bay reported an all-time record. They'd taken 45.8 million fish—25.8 million of which had been destined for the Kvichak River. The escapement into Iliamna amounted to only 3.5 million salmon. The commercial fishermen had netted 81% of the entire Kvichak run—instead of three out of every four fish, this year the commercial harvest had taken more than four out of five.

In mid-July, I telephoned first the biologists in King Salmon and then the commissioner's office in Juneau to protest the protracted commercial season. With a record return into the Bay, and a record harvest developing, more fish should have made it into Lake Iliamna.

"We understand your concern, Ted," one official said, "but I can't really help you. The Kvichak has already received its target of 2 million fish."

"That was set last winter, before we knew about this huge run of fish."

"I'm sorry. The board set the target at 2 million and we can't change it now."

"You didn't hesitate to lower the target last year when the run failed to materialize!" I argued, but I could see it was a losing battle. The ADFG was shooting for an all-time harvest record in Bristol Bay—and to hell with conservation efforts and increased escapements for future years. This same philosophy had already devastated the stocks of king crab, shrimp, and herring in other areas of the state and it was now destined to devastate the salmon in Bristol Bay, but no one seemed to care.

It was time to send the commissioner another broadside describing conditions on the Copper and Iliamna rivers. "While the commercial fishermen in Bristol Bay are enjoying a record catch," I wrote, "our sport fishing industry is starving... Our own state record in management has left much to be desired, when we look at the herring industry of Prince William Sound and Kodiak, shrimp fishery of Kodiak, king crab fisheries of Kodiak and Bristol Bay, and king salmon returns to Cook Inlet. Now these same biologists are telling us it's all right to harvest over 75% of the Bristol Bay sockeye salmon runs. Nonsense!"

That letter he never answered. When the commercial season closed and the fishermen returned home, I asked several of them about the 1983 season. To a man, they all agreed that the escapement should have been higher and that the season shouldn't have remained open so long.

I talked to Pat Poe, the local fisheries biologist in charge of the Lake Iliamna section of the Fisheries Research Institute, an arm of the University of Washington. Pat was an old hand on the lake, thoroughly versed in the life cycle of the sockeye salmon, which he had been studying for many years. He agreed with the rest of us that the ADFG managers should have allowed a greater escapement in view of the huge run of salmon into the Bay.

In July, confident that the advisory committee would support me, I decided to submit my own proposal to the board. After documenting my case, I proposed that: "Escapement targets for sockeye salmon shall be a minimum of one half of the total number of salmon returning to the Bristol Bay drainages each year. Particular emphasis shall be placed on meeting this target for the Kvichak River."

In October I flew to Anchorage to stop by the regional fish and game office on Raspberry Road. I spoke first with the supervisor in charge of sport fishing, who sympathized but could do little to help. Next I spoke with the director of the Commercial Fish Division in his small office on the second floor.

"I'd like to talk about Bristol Bay sockeye salmon escapement policy," I said.

"Sure, Ted. I recognize your concern," he said. He was a man approaching 50 and tending toward baldness. "I've been reading some of your letters to the commissioner."

"Why didn't your managers in King Salmon allow a greater escapement last summer?" I asked.

"Our records show that the Kvichak received 3.5 million fish," he said. "You were only targeted for 2 million. I wouldn't consider that small."

"It was a huge return," I argued. "A higher percentage of fish should have been allowed to escape. Even the commercial fishermen in Iliamna agree, as well as some of your own biologists."

"But I don't agree!" he said—and right there I knew I'd found the man who'd deliberately kept the commercial season open. He probably felt a record harvest would look good on his own management record.

"Have you seen the proposal I submitted to the board?" I asked. "It requires a minimum escapement of at least half the return each year."

Not only had he heard about my proposal, he was violently opposed to it. "If they adopt that proposal, there won't be any need for biologists any more. Technicians could handle everything."

223

"Technicians couldn't have done any worse than you biologists the past three years!" I said—and left another ADFG biologist's office with heartburn and an upset stomach. The worst predator on our fish stocks in Bristol Bay were apparently the managers hired to conserve the species!

I heard from the Board of Fisheries in November. They refused to consider my proposal because, they said, their winter agenda was already too full and the situation I'd described wasn't "of critical biological importance."

Just before Christmas I got a note from Pat Poe advising me that all the biologists involved in the management program for Bristol Bay sockeye salmon were gathering to restudy the current plan and would meet in King Salmon in January. He knew I'd want to attend. That very evening, I wrote to the commissioner requesting an invitation.

Three weeks later the commissioner's office advised me that the staff meeting at King Salmon was for professional biologists to review scientific information and develop escapement goals to present to the board. "Your comments and suggestions would be more appropriate during the February Board of Fisheries meeting," he wrote. In other words, we don't want you and your ideas in King Salmon!

"What are they afraid of?" I asked Mary after reading the letter. "Why not at least listen to me? Who has a better idea what goes on upstream than I do? I'm out there every day—I haven't seen a state fish and game biologist here in five years."

"At least you tried," she answered.

"Tried hell! I'm going anyway," I said.

"Telephone first," Mary suggested. "At least let them know you're coming."

"I'll do that much," I said. "The meeting's next week."

On the first day of their meeting, I received a call from the chairman of the study group. "Hello, Ted," he introduced himself. "This is Ken Florey in King Salmon returning your call."

I recognized the name. Ken was one of the biologists in the Anchorage office. "I was tipped off about your meeting on sockeye salmon," I said. "I'd like to come down at a convenient time for you and address the group."

"You're welcome to come, of course. I was going to give you a call anyway because I think you'll be interested in what we've come up with so far."

"I'm listening," I said. I didn't trust any scheme of any fish and game biologist.

"It looks like we'll be recommending a substantial change in the management plan for Bristol Bay sockeye salmon to the board next month. Our thoughts now are to try and level out the runs from year to year. We'll recommend allowing additional harvest during the peak and pre-peak part of the cycle but restrict the harvest more during the low-cycle years."

"How much of a restriction?" I wanted to know.

"Looks like we'll try for a minimum escapement of four to five million up the Kvichak during low years and 8 to 10 million during the peaks."

I couldn't believe it. After years of effort, frustration, and rage, he was finally telling me what I wanted to hear!

"Sounds like you fellows are finally starting to get the picture," I said. "Thanks for calling. You don't need me there now."

Mary couldn't believe it either, but she joined me in dancing around the living room. "You did it, Ted. You really did it!" she exclaimed.

"I doubt it. The commercial fishermen had a record catch last year, and they're probably having a hard time selling all the salmon still in their warehouses. They probably want to restrict the harvest because fewer fish mean higher prices."

"Don't sell yourself short, Ted Gerken," Mary said. "You made an impact. Who says you can't fight city hall?"

"Maybe," I conceded. "Maybe the managers at Fish and Game have finally realized the effects of overharvesting. Maybe they're even becoming a little more conservative with what's left. Maybe. We'll see."

CHAPTER 41

T he sockeye salmon escapements into the Kvichak River were 10.4 million fish in 1984 but only 7.2 million in 1985. The biologists had been trying to adhere to their new plan in 1985, but intercept of Kvichak stocks along Bristol Bay had been larger than they'd expected. As a result, the state is continuing to study the matter, now calling for suggestions from the advisory committees and anyone else interested in the fishery.

They started a testing program in 1985 to attempt to identify each sub-species of salmon by river of origin. Teams of biologists established test fisheries within each commercial fishing zone in Bristol Bay. They took scale samples of each fish and, later that season, compared them to scales taken from dead fish found along the spawning rivers within each drainage. Their preliminary analysis indicated that the commercial fishermen harvest a disproportionate number of Kvichak-bound salmon while the fish are still in the Bay. In the Naknek district alone, Kvichak fish comprised about 25% of their catch, with smaller but significant lesser percentages showing up in the Egegik and Ugashik districts.

If these few preliminary tests can be trusted to reflect actual harvest conditions, the state biologists may have finally hit on the real problem—almost 40% of the annual return of Kvichak-bound fish is being harvested in other fishing districts. By restricting the harvest within these other districts, there's a good chance that the large runs of the past can be re-established in the Kvichak.

Iliaska Lodge now operates two Cessna 206s on floats, a Dehavilland Beaver on floats, and a Piper PA12 three-place airplane mounted on oversized tundra tires. We have a dozen jet-powered outboards that we leave on rivers throughout the area each summer. We take only twelve fly-fishing guests at the lodge each week.

I'm still flying and Mary still cooks breakfast each morning. Her jaw has now gone through two years of orthodontics, and it hasn't locked shut since that first time in 1979. She obtained her private pilot's license in April, 1986. We close up shop in October and don't open again until the following June.

In the 1984 general election, the Alaska Transportation Commission was voted out of existence, so there's no longer any state regulation of transportation in Alaska. The village of Iliamna now has commercial power—but we keep our generator in operating condition just in case. There's still a number of power outages each year. The village now has one television channel provided by the state.

Among the many improvements we've made to the lodge over the past 12 years is a two-story, 800-square-foot addition off the front room; we use the upper floor as a dining room and the basement for the crew. We built Mary a greenhouse off the southwest side of the addition.

Uncle Bill has made it back to Alaska 16 years in a row—and still counting. During that time he has developed several fly patterns for sockeye and silver salmon that are now part of our lodge inventory.

As for our children, on January 9, 1984, in Anchorage Superior Court, Angela and Elizabeth formally adopted me as their father and took the surname Gerken. Angie is now a junior at the University of Alaska in Fairbanks majoring in Russian Studies, with a minor in Education. Liz is a senior in high school at Homer, Alaska (the southernmost town on the road that runs down the Kenai Peninsula), where Mary and I now spend our winters.

Our eldest son Bill graduated from Chaminade University in Honolulu in 1985 with a degree in Computer Science and is now running his own computer consulting company in Anchorage. On Valentine's day, 1988, his wife Karin gave birth to a baby girl—making me a grandfather. Our youngest son David graduated from the University of Hawaii in December 1986, with a degree in Zoology and is now training dolphins, sea lions, and false killer whales at Sea Life Park on the island of Oahu. A scholarship has been established at Kodiak High School in memory of Tom and his friends.

Our gamble at Iliamna has paid off in many ways. My dream to fly, hunt, fish, and explore the grandeur of Alaska to my heart's content has been fulfilled, and Mary accompanies me on as many of these trips as possible. But it is the myriad number of friends we have introduced to Alaska that makes it so much more rewarding. There's hardly another state in the Union that Mary and I can now visit without finding at least one fly-fisherman who has fished with us at Iliaska, many of whom have returned several times over the years. The Book, established in 1979 to record significant catches of fish by our guests and guides documents the accomplishments of these repeaters: Bob Johnson, an attorney from Encino, California, has made it nine years in a row, and recorded several entries such as "4 July, 1980 - Independence Day for the trout on the Copper River! Approximately 200 fish were caught by Ted Gerken, Fred Brainerd, Milt Huber, John Meade and myself. Some fish to four pounds or better, using Grizzly Wulff, Black Wulff, Black Gnat, Adams, and Deschutes Stone Fly. All on DRY FLIES!"

Harm Saville, a renowned miniature rose horticulturist from Rowley, Massachusetts, recorded this entry: "September 28, 1980, Lower Talarik Creek rainbow trout 30-1/2", 11-1/2#, Ugly Fly (leech pattern variation)."

Wayne Poulsen of Squaw Valley, California, made several exploration trips with me in the early 1980s. He made this entry on June 9th, 1981: "Exploration day on the upper Copper (above Fog Lake). Dave and Ted Gerken, Wayne Poulsen had the best day in anyone's memory - average 4# plus! Up to 7#

rainbows in fantastic numbers on maribou sculpin streamers."

Gerry Smith raises sheep in Litchfield, Connecticut, and has been bringing several friends with him each year since 1981. A true sportsman who enjoys a challenge, he recorded this entry on June 20th, 1985: "Iliamna River - many fish feeding on fry but very hard to catch. Finally tried a new fly tied by our guide Chuck Kramer the night before—in three casts took a 6 and 7 1/2 pound char."

Ed Ruestow, the president of Clapp and Treat, a large sporting goods store in West Hartford, Connecticut, has made six trips to the lodge. Ed prefers the larger fish available in August and September and recorded the following for his group: "31 August, 1987. Volcano Creek—the most outstanding day of fishing anyone could have. Approximately 100 silver salmon taken by four fishermen, averaging over 10 pounds and up to 16. Clear sunny day, 65 degrees, one bear. White leeches and everything else worked. Four Star!"

The list goes on and on—over 2,000 Book entries now, most of them a record of multiple catches. The Book is not only a record of how well individuals have done, but of greater importance, a documentary on the relative health of each species of fish and each stream we have fished for the past nine years. It will be a valuable research document should I find myself in another dispute with the Alaska Department of Fish and Game. We started volume two in 1988.

By recognizing but a few fishing guests, I run the risk of slighting the many others who have contributed greatly to our success. It is inappropriate to name all thousand who have fished with us, plus the second thousand who dropped in for coffee, dinner, or lodging those first years. But it would be a shame not to mention George Lower of Gettysburg, Pennsylvania, a guest sent to us by Thomas and Thomas of Turner's Falls, Massachusetts. George was so enamored of the lodge that after three visits in successive years as a guest, he sold his Civil War antique business, retired, and now guides other fishermen for us in the summer and helps with advertising in the winter.

The quiet streams full of fish; the stark, snow-capped mountains; the endless tundra; the timbered valleys and sparkling lakes—the immense and unpopulated wilderness of Alaska has brought adventurous men and women north for centuries. It continues to hold us here. There's no other place like it.